THE BRITISH CAVALRY SWORD FROM 1600

THE BRITISH CAVALRY SWORD FROM 1600

Charles Martyn

Pen & Sword
MILITARY

First published in Great Britain in 2004 by
Pen & Sword Military
an imprint of
Pen & Sword Books Ltd
47 Church Street
Barnsley
South Yorkshire
S70 2AS

ISBN 1-84415-071-2

A CIP catalogue record for this book is
available from the British Library

Typeset in Palatino

Printed and bound in Great Britain by CPI UK

For a complete list of Pen & Sword titles, please contact
Pen & Sword Books Limited
47 Church Street, Barnsley, South Yorkshire, S70 2AS, England
E-mail: enquiries@pen-and-sword.co.uk
Website: www.pen-and-sword.co.uk

Contents

GLOSSARY

SWORD TERMS AND EXPRESSIONS

PARTS OF THE HILT

Backstrap	A metallic cover at the back of the grip that may also form the pommel.
3-Bar	Where the guard is built up from two curved bars and a knucklebow.
4-Bar	Similarly, the guard is built up from three curved bars and a knucklebow.
Ferrule	A strong metal ring, usually ovoid, which holds the grip about the tang.
Fish skin	The skin of a fish, usually dogfish or shark that has a slip-free surface and can be used as the outer covering of the grip.
Grip	The materials covering or riveted to the tang that enable the sword to be held comfortably.
Guard	Metal that is formed around the grip to protect the hand.
Knopple	A bulbous area in the bar of a guard.
Knucklebow	A simple guard of one bar that gives limited protection across the hand knuckles.
Pommel	Usually a solid casting of varying shape that can be screwed or peened to the tang to secure the grip and ferrules against the step of the blade tang.
Turks-head	A braided wire at the top and bottom of the grip, in place of ferrules, but for a decorative function.

PARTS OF THE BLADE

The blade may be described as the exposed length of the sword that has a cutting edge or thrusting point.

Back-edge	A flat or rounded edge at the back of the blade.
Broadsword	Usually describes a blade that is double edged.
Cross-section	The shape of the transverse section of the blade.
Forte	The short length of blade upon which the grip and guard rest, usually rectangular in cross-section and which may also be used for armourers or manufacturing marks and for inserting the proof mark.
Fuller	A depression over the lengths of the blade to decrease weight, but retain strength; also allows for easier withdrawal after thrusting.

| Pipe-back | A cylindrical section at the back of a blade to decrease flexibility of the blade. |
| Tang | An extension of the blade that becomes the covered length to accommodate the grip, guard, pommel and ferrules. |

GENERAL EXPRESSIONS

Celtic	In the manner of Celtic designs and decorations.
Recurving	Curving from one direction into the opposite direction.
Saltire	The Scottish cross of two diagonals.
Saxon	Sword types derived from Saxony, from the early sixteenth century.
Walloon	A general term for the area inhabited by the Flemish, Dutch and Belgian people from the sixteenth century.

ABBREVIATIONS

ADC	Aide-de-Camp.
AN	The general prefix adopted by the French in numbering the patterns for their swords after the revolution. E.g. AN. XII.
Brig	Brigadier - an Army rank.
c.	Circa, or, from about this time.
CLY.	County of London Yeomanry.
cm.	Centimetre
ECYC	Earl of Chester's Yeomanry Cavalry.
EFD	Enfield (small arms factory.)
EIC	East India Company.
EKMR	East Kent Mounted Rifles.
ERI	Edward Rex Imperator (Edward VII.)
Exp	Experimental.
FKY	Fife & Kinross Yeomanry.
GOC	General Officer Commanding.
GR	George Rex (applicable to George I, II, III & IV.)
GRI	George Rex Imperator (George V.)
H	Hussars.
HC or H/C	Household Cavalry.
Hon	Honourable (refers to a Chartered Company.)
I	Could refer to an Inspection mark.
ISD	Indian Stores Department.
IY	Imperial Yeomanry.
Kg	Kilograms
L	Lancer (s)
Lb	Pound (s) in weight.

LC	Light Cavalry.
LG	Life Guards.
MI	Mounted Infantry.
Mil	Military.
Oz	Ounce (s) in weight.
P or Patt	Pattern.
QLD	Queen's Light Dragoons.
QOCH	Queen's Own Cameron Highlanders.
RHG	Royal Horse Guards.
SALH	South African Light Horse.
VR	Victoria Regina.
Wm IV	William IV.
WYC	Warwickshire Yeomanry Cavalry.
Yeo	Yeomanry.

ACKNOWLEDGEMENTS

Due acknowledgements and credits are given to the following authors and organizations:

P.G.W. Annis; C.R.B. Barratt; David Blackmore; Charles Ffoulkes; E.C. Hopkinson; Frederick Leary; Elizabeth Longford; Lieutenant Commander W.E. May; G.I. Mungeam; George C. Neumann; A.V.B. Norman; Thomas Pakenham; Brian Robson; John Walter; Frederick Wilkinson.

Household Cavalry Museum, Windsor; 4th/7th Dragoon Guards Museum, York; 17th/21st Lancers RHQ, Grantham; The Pattern Room, Enfield; The Tower of London; The Arms and Armour Society; The Wilkinson Sword Co. Ltd; Wallis & Wallis, specialist Military Auctioneers, Lewes; Littlecote House; Rufford Old Hall (National Trust); York Castle Museum; Warwick Castle.

Cheryl A. Biden, who willingly prepared the first presentation for the publisher.

My daughter Virginia, for her continual support.

ABOUT THIS BOOK

Why do people collect anything at all? The answers to this are diverse and very much dependent upon the nature of the person. Some people are natural hoarders and collectors of something or other; some need their collection for display and to emerge as part of the environment of their home. Some use a collection as a follow up interest originating from their profession. These days, more people are looking at antiques and the older 'unlicensed' arms as a means of investment and temporary interest. Apart from these reasons, and the many more that one could find, we should perhaps explore a few more ordered motives that highlight the subject under consideration.

A simple definition of 'to collect' could be 'to assemble or bring together', even 'to put one's thoughts in order', or 'to infer', which itself means 'to derive as a consequence or arrive at a logical conclusion'. These individual references when combined, are the basic reasons for pulling together a collection of British Cavalry Swords. The collector could well be led on to further areas of associated interest and diverse activities of research.

The subject of British Cavalry swords is by no means complete and defined. For example, the formal patterns were started in the 1780s but not always complied with, consequently, variations to a pattern, (or the individual requirements of some officers) over a period of about 130 years, are considerable. The British Cavalry sword is admirably suited as an *objet trouvé* for there are a number of approaches to the hobby. Swords may be collected by regiment, from formation to recent amalgamation, or by specific type or pattern, or variations of a pattern. You have to bear in mind that these weapons are a matter of history and will never be repeated in any future British army as a fighting weapon. You will doubtless be led on to research the battles in which a particular type was employed.

In the first steps of collecting you should accumulate a general appreciation of the subject. This can be gained from reading works already published. A bibliography of suitable books is included. These books cover swords in general, and only partly deal with cavalry weapons. Nevertheless, they are authoritative and will provide some background and essential information. There may be some variances which should not be ignored as these will contribute to your own interpretation of the subject, and your own collection, but will have been based upon the information available to that author at that time. Unfortunately, some of these books will be out of print, and may only be available from specialist sources or auctions of militaria. In this respect, this book has taken a few of the earlier areas of interest that could be expanded and recounted by taking the existing information made available to the public, and relating it to the examples illustrated, together with any other information into one interpretable package that will give some authenticity into what may have been debatable or vague. An example of this is shown in Chapter 3.

Having absorbed the information from the books, particularly that relating to identification of British cavalry swords, which is principally by the form of the hilt (but bearing in mind that all horse-borne regiments of artillery, yeomanry, transport and even mounted infantry all used the equivalent cavalry sword) you then should visit those regimental museums and historic houses that could be associated with this subject to familiarize yourself with those forms and points of identification. This point is pursued in this book where a few existing examples are quoted, together with the year in which they were observed. The reason for the date being noted is that many museums change their content over a period of time, so something noted in 1971 may not be seen in 2003.

Since the Second World War, the cavalry regiments have been amalgamated beyond recognition, and consequently the regimental museums have had to cater for this; not only amalgamations taking place periodically, but the Ministry of Defence selling off many of its properties where collections may have been stored has exacerbated the overall situation. The keen researcher, trying to find out details of an officer's record of service, may find that they are no longer at the regimental museum, but at some totally different storage area as an interim. This situation will settle out in time.

Cavalry swords are available for purchase through a number of sources: dealers in militaria, specialist dealers in arms, specialist auctioneers in arms, antique and trade fairs, private transactions with other collectors and sometimes, even by visiting junk shops. Prices will vary. Each of these sources will have a degree of expertise to offer whilst selling, but your own judgement and need is the main consideration when buying, providing you are satisfied with what you have bought. Prominent dealers and auctioneers will provide descriptive catalogues with photographs so that you can reasonably determine the types of swords and their physical state, but this is no guarantee. In general, no sword can be in a perfect state. Swords which have seen active service, particularly those used in the Crimea and Napoleonic Wars inevitably show the effects of their usage and the environmental conditions.

Having bought a sword, whatever the condition, do not subject it to any form of abrasive cleaning. This will leave score marks that may be difficult to remove, and even possibly reveal some underlying defect. Worst of all, abrasive cleaning is likely to remove a well established patina, the decorative features, and any identification features such as manufacturers' and suppliers' details, viewing and inspection marks, and thence the provenance. What you should do is regularly wax polish (the latest is crystalline wax) the surfaces, and wax again whenever it has been handled. This will maintain the sword, provide a light protective surface and enhance its appearance without defacing its value.

The provenance of original ownership may be difficult to establish, but may also depend upon how far you want to take it. The purchased sword may be provided with some provenance by the seller. Failing that, provenance may be traced through documents and histories such as family crests, coats of arms or *Burke's Peerage*, or similar records. Another way to establish provenance is by a stamped number (now probably only relevant to swords manufactured by Wilkinson). Also Army Lists, regimental histories, service histories and references from regimental museums. There are even published instances of a particular sword's wartime employment. Seeking out a blade's history can be a slow laborious process. Such was the case with the sword of Major C.H. Villiers covered in Chapters 10 and 15 of this book, spread over a period of two years, involving an initial provenance from Wilkinsons. This was followed by a search through *Kelly's Handbook to the Titled, Landed and Official Classes* of 1911, *Debrett's Peerage* of 1928, a service history afforded by the Household Cavalry Museum, and two accounts from *Jameson's Raid* by Elizabeth Longford, and *The Boer War* by Thomas Pakenham. Nevertheless, it was satisfying work, and the net result was to establish that a particular sword was a piece of British military history.

A few last words before you go off finding your collection. It is advisable that once you start collecting, your purchases should be catalogued with a full description, price and place of purchase, and provenances as they are obtained. These should be accompanied by photographs. This simple procedure has advantages for insurance, identification to the police if stolen, as well as making a complete history of each sword. If your collection progresses over a long period of time, it would also be a good idea to periodically note the escalatory costs of types and patterns, as this may help you in future pricing of prospective purchases, and even give indications of rarity and availablity.

Welcome to the world of collecting!

INTRODUCTION

It is difficult to say who or when the principle of the knife, and its logical follower the sword, was first recognized and developed. Whether of flint, bronze or iron, the cutting edge and sharp point were borne out of necessity for hunting, clothing and survival. Given the remoteness of one culture from another, the evolvement from knife to sword, was more or less simultaneous in each culture, the differences in the forms of the sword being guided by the environment and characteristics of the culture. While Europe's crusaders used a cross guarded broadsword, their Muslim opponents adopted the mameluke hilted curved sword which was lighter and easier to wield in the skirmish. The common component of these two vastly different swords was the simple cross guard fitted above the blade to prevent the hand slipping over the blade, but also to give some limited protection to the hand in taking or intercepting an opponent's cut.

In Europe the cross guard hilted sword remained in existence for perhaps 1,000 years, the principles maintained as a double edged blade, the tang of which was bound and covered to form a grip, the hand restrained to the grip by the guard at the blade forte and by the rear mounted pommel. This was a simple enough and very effective weapon used by both foot and horse soldiers alike.

There was little difference between swords used for fighting on foot or by horse; perhaps those who were horse borne used longer blades. There was a difference in the forms of the guard and pommel, these differences being used as a means of identifying the region of origin (for example the extended diamond form of the guard quillons as shown in Fig.1 is generally accepted as of North European Saxon origin); or to the owner by his markings on the pommel.

The pommel also had a secondary function particularly for the horse borne soldier, that of being used for fighting when blade movement was restricted and, therefore, effective only through its weight and solidity. In time the form and design of swords were influenced by outside factors: increasing trade; importation from more cognizant armourers abroad; the use by foreign mercenaries; and acquiring foreign swords in battle, not only as individual trophies, but, more importantly, to extend an army's arsenal. Then there were the local armouries maintained by the knights and nobility licensed to raise levies and war bands. Some of these practices continued well into the eighteenth century until the Boards of

Possible sequence in basket guard development

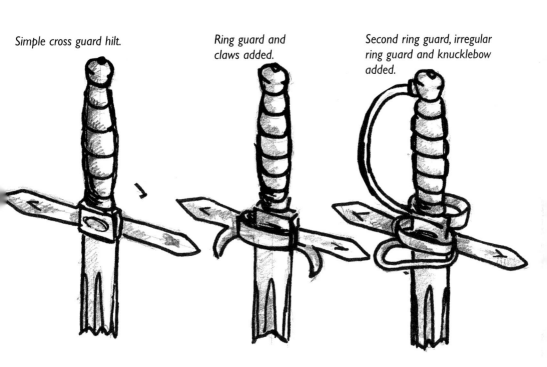

Simple cross guard hilt.

Ring guard and claws added.

Second ring guard, irregular ring guard and knucklebow added.

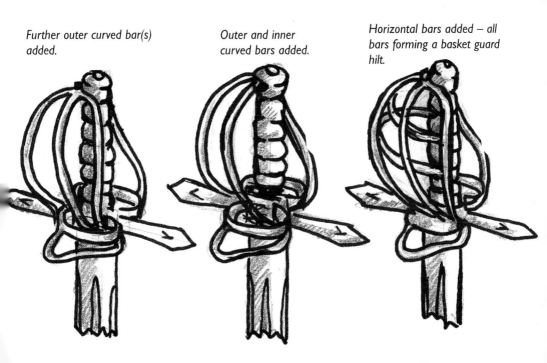

Further outer curved bar(s) added.

Outer and inner curved bars added.

Horizontal bars added – all bars forming a basket guard hilt.

Ordnance established the need for consistency and a degree of fitness for purpose in all British service weapons. In these circumstances the weapons acquired became British by right and by use, irrespective of place of origin, manufacture or form, each reason contributing to a change or an advancement in sword development.

Irrespective of their relative simplicity, swords have always been expensive to produce and were never manufactured in large quantities at any one time (an exception being the 1796 light cavalry sabre which was produced in the thousands during the Napoleonic wars, and which can be found today in many private collections and military museums all over Great Britain and Europe).

Swords were mainly the prerogative of the nobility; knights, commanders and men-at-arms, all men who were trained and excelled in their use. Their relative scarcity made them highly prized possessions, and their owners were accordingly noted by honour and leadership. The form of the cross hilted broadsword only began to differ once tactics of battles changed, and the horse soldier began to lose his armour. Even this process was extremely slow, and still subject to outside influences of those regions more experienced in the arts of war, and improved techniques of manufacture. The principal changes, and additions, were those made necessary to protect the hand, it eventually being recognized that the rudimentary cross guard was no longer a protection against a cut across the hand. It was no longer relevant in a world where the swordsman was becoming more accomplished in his art, and other forms of protection had to be found to compensate for the absence of associated armour.

These changes and additions took place on the sword itself and did not necessarily follow logical sequences, but a reasonable logical sequence may be seen on page 13. These diagrams show the transformation from the cross guard hilt to a form of full basket hilt that would give cover to most of the hand.

Any work on swords, particularly those used by the cavalry, can only attempt to show a sequence or a history of their form and their changes. This book alone portrays over forty forms of cavalry sword hilt that have not been shown in previous and existing works. A hidden store of other cavalry swords is held in military museums, historic houses, and private collections that may never come to light unless they are sought out, researched and published. This book attempts to increase the knowledge of the British Cavalry sword, but is a work which can be further extended as the history unfolds.

Chapter 1

LATTER SIXTEENTH CENTURY

The inevitable changes to the principle of the simple cross guard sword, (which was formed from a straight double edged blade mounted with a large pommel, grip and cross guard), were slow to evolve, only taking place in the late fourteenth century and continuing through into the late sixteenth century. Whilst the length of the blade varied considerably from 21in (53.5cm) to 40in (101.5cm), and the hand-and-a-half swords would have extended to 50in (127cm), the horseman's sword rarely exceeded the 40in dimension and adhered to the broadsword form, although generally of lighter weight. The changes were more apparent in the hilt through the incorporation of additional guards to the hilt and through the eventual realization that the simple cross guard was totally inadequate for protection from the increasing demands of contemporary warfare.

Protection to the hand that wielded the sword was essential, more so by the need to compensate for the lightening or loss of armour. Then there was the need to be counter aggressive against the expert swordsman by deflecting or trapping his blade. These requirements led to the construction of a surrounding guard about the grip and the hand. Now it is commonly referred to as a basket guard.

Towards the end of the sixteenth century two significant developments had taken place using these safeguards which were to shape the progress and future of both heavy and light cavalry swords of the British Army.

Full Basket Hilted Broadsword c. 1570
Illustrations 1(i) and 1(ii)

These portray two opposing views of a sword hilt c.1570 directly evolved from the Saxon (Northern Germany) medieval cross hilted sword. The enlarged pyramidal pommel, chiselled with random scrolling, typical of sixteenth century decoration, was sufficient in both size and weight to be used forcibly for fighting where it was not possible to use the blade. The grip was of close bound iron wire around iron bars fitted about the blade tang, and pressed to form a classical columnar effect. The lattice form basket is distinctive for its time, constructed from vertical and diagonal bars hot hammered together, the joins sealed with the Scottish Saltire, the basket being built up from an ovoid ring on one side and an interconnecting irregular ring on the other. To give added hand control of the weapon the irregular ring has an integral thumbgrip. The blade is of broadsword form, tapering, and flattened hexagonal in cross section, marked from the forte with the word, or name 'IVANI', and an armourer's mark of a diamond with a cross.

Blade length	33.5in (85cm)
Sword weight	2lb 7oz (1.12 kg)

This form of lattice basket guard was repeated in cavalry swords of the seventeenth and eighteenth centuries.

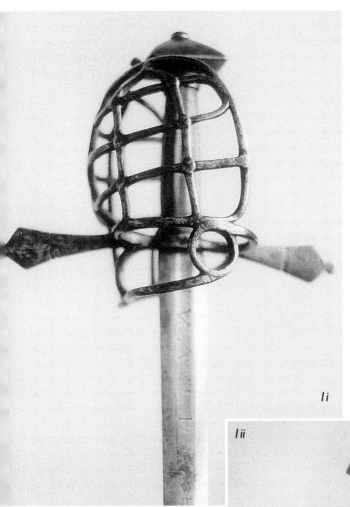

*Full basket hilted
broadsword c. 1570*

I i

I ii

Sinclair sabel c. 1570

2i

2ii

Sinclair Sabel c. 1570
Illustrations 2(i) and 2(ii)

The opposing views of the hilt of a 'Sinclair Sabel', c. 1570, the second significant development, which was brought about by joint Scottish and northern European endeavours. The initial influences for this sword came from the Middle Eastern crusades, and later from the Mongol invasion of Eastern Europe. The main arm of these fast moving horsemen was a curved sharp sword for cutting on the move; a tactic which became highly developed by Eastern European countries as far north as the Baltic seaboard, and developed into the light sabre or 'sabel', and the eventual formation of light cavalry units in most European and British armies.

The Sinclair Sabel has been defined as a curved sword with a triangular hilt. This effect may be seen in two planes, but only if one allows that the basket construction bars are curved and not straight; otherwise the view is hemispherical about the hand. The quillons (cross guard) and pyramidal pommel are of Saxon influence. The grip is made from cord wound around the tang and covered in leather, and is only 3in (75mm) in length. The lower end of the pommel is shaped to give a comfortable but tight fit to the hand within the basket. The basket guard of broad bulbous bars is built up from the quillons, an ovoid side ring and an opposing irregular ring with thumb grip as portrayed in the first example. The curved bars of the basket are, in practice, a knucklebow, and two opposing diagonals. The blade is curved, single-edged and broad fullered, with a false edge of 9.8in (25cm) and slightly clipped at the point; one side is plain, the other side has an armourer's mark of a fleur-de-lis over 'W' set in a line of five 'cogs'.

Blade length	33in (84cm)
Blade weight	0.93Kg (2lb 1oz)

Sinclair hilted broadsword c. 1580
Illustration 3

Much of Britain's historical and military background is still within the confines of its historic houses either owned by the nobility and middle class entrepreneurs, or those now run and maintained by national enterprises. One such house is Rufford Old Hall in Lancashire, one time family home of the Heskeths, but now run by the National Trust. One can find there a small, but not insignificant collection of arms and armour, including a possibly unique example of a Sinclair hilted broadsword c.1580. By the general form of the German blade, which tapers over its length (approximately 42in 106.7cm) into a secondary 'back edge' of about 9in (23cm) towards the point, this sword is ideal for the horsemen and cavalry action of the period.

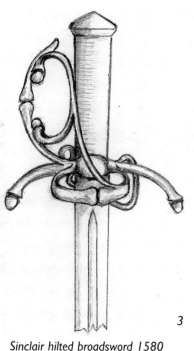

Sinclair hilted broadsword 1580

Open basket hilted broadsword

The hilt is of open basket construction based upon the medieval form of the cross guard with downward curving quillons and acorn finials, an outer ring guard, and an inner irregular bar guard. The open basket is constructed from a curved knucklebow (not connected to the pommel), a diagonal curved bar down to the ring guard, and a medial re-curving bar. The bars are decorated with an acorn finial and an early form of 'knoppels' as used on the later Walloon swords.

Open Basket Hilt Broadsword
Illustration 4

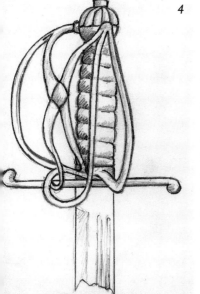

This is representative of some horseman's swords in a form that was probably developed from the middle of the sixteenth century from Scottish and possibly Irish influences, but was most prominent at the end of the century. The bars of the basket are vertical, interconnected with diagonals and small diamond shaped panels, generally dispersed equally about the grip to form an all-round open basket hilt.

CHAPTER 2

THE SEVENTEENTH CENTURY

In Britain of the early 1600s there was a state of relative peace, the effects of war only being felt by those English and Scottish mercenaries and adventurers who contracted with the Dutch and German states for the constant skirmishes that were taking place in Europe at that time. The development of the horseman or cavalry sword in Britain, however, was far from static. With the adoption of the various forms of the Dutch and Walloon cavalry swords that the mercenaries had encountered, and which were becoming basic tools in the embryonic cavalry units leading into the Thirty Years War; the open basket hilt to reflect the characteristics of the heavy Walloon cuirassiers sword; but also to take a new approach, that of economy and ease of manufacture to produce a 'skeletal' form of open basket. A number of conventional adaptations were made from other existing swords such as the swept, cup-hilt and scallop shell guards of the rapier; neither was it unusual to use grips of antler horn or other natural materials where the raised surfaces provided a natural non-slip condition for the manipulation of the sword.

The Thirty Years War in Europe began in 1618; a brutal war that devastated Central Europe. Of religious origins between Catholics and the Protestants within the disintegrating Holy Roman Empire, it was also a war of power succession, fuelled by the opposing catholic kingdoms of Spain and France, and latterly by the Protestant kingdoms of Sweden and Denmark in support of the protestant 'ethnic' minorities. It was a war of ever changing tactics, objectives and sides; Britain did not join the fight, except for some minor incursions to show support of Frederick, Elector of the Palatine, and son-in-law to James I. A high proportion of the armies employed by the major states in this conflict were mercenary; the English, Scottish, Welsh and Irish well to the fore, to suit their religious following, or simply for the best offer. Mercenaries came and went, taking their experience and their weapons back to their own country, especially in Britain, where, as the Thirty Years War went into decline, the Civil War of 1642 erupted. Once again the Walloon swords had come into their own for cavalry use, in particular a lightweight sword, which was soon to be anglicized and continue in British cavalry service through to the middle of the eighteenth century.

At the commencement of the Civil War in Britain, when Charles I fled London, he unwittingly left the London and Hounslow weapon manufacturers in the hands of the Puritans. Cromwell seized the arsenal at Cambridge within a matter of days, and both these situations gave a distinct advantage to the Puritans. With the Royalists spread over the country as separate entities, and no formal base (until Oxford much later) from which to organize or form manufacturing centres, they were left only with their own personal arms and equipment, often outdated and not suitable for cavalry use, and could only renew their equipment by importation through their royal connections in Holland. Despite these restrictions, the Royalists fought and gained many notable battles, but were not finally able to counter the efficiency of the organization set up by the Puritan general command. Even though the Puritans had access to the main manufactures to produce 'pattern' swords such as the proto-mortuary and mortuary swords for cavalry use, they also appear to have eventually encountered production problems for sufficient supply; G.I. Mungeam in *Contracts for the supply of Equipment to the New Model Army in 1645* records that during that year orders were placed with British suppliers for 11,600 swords, of which 2,400 were specifically to have Dutch blades. Two hundred were to be for horsemen. This account sadly reflects upon the ability, or availability, of British craftsmen, particularly when even the shovels were specified to be of Dutch manufacture. However, the advantage that Fairfax established with the formation of the New Model Army was that all weapons were produced to recognized standards of consistency and fitness of purpose, the first attempt in Britain to control arms production.

With the restoration and accession of Charles II, the strict regimes established by Fairfax became considerably relaxed; from 1661 the cavalry sword hilt began to change yet again to reflect the expansive era of royal reign through to the end of the century.

Early Walloon Broadsword c. 1610
Illustrations 5 and 6

These show the general form and construction of the early Walloon broadsword which took the notice of the mercenaries contracted to the Dutch and German States at the beginning of the century and which became anglicized for British horsemen c. 1610; a form that with variants continued through to c.1740. The medieval cross-guard is in effect retained but acting only as a stiffener in construction across a diamond or square shaped plate. This has been formed into a dish of which the inner and outer edges are raised to give some protection to the hand; the forward and rear points combining with the stiffener as small recurving quillons.

The distinctive knucklebow with two recurving branches between the baseguard and the pommel is a further feature of Walloon swords which recurs on the anglicized swords. The English sword featured in the illustration has a grip covered in fine copper wire, overbound by a fine roped copper wire, and secured top and bottom with copper wire Turks Heads.

Hilt decoration is by simple chiselled marks on the knucklebow and striations on the outside of the dish, vaguely representative of foliage and shell formations. The blade is elliptical in cross-section with a central fuller of 7in (17.75cm) length, tapering over its entire length. Although considerably worn, the blade shows residual Running Wolf marks, and 'point' decoration in the fuller.

Blade length	34.25in (87cm)
Sword weight	1lb 13oz (0.83kg)

A sword of this type is displayed at Chirk Castle.

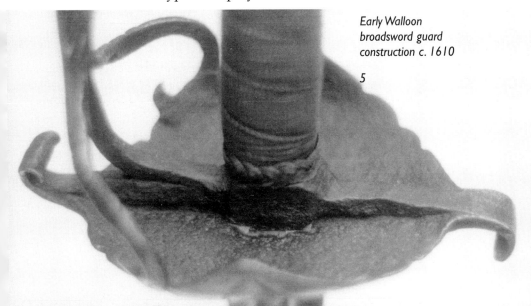

Early Walloon broadsword guard construction c. 1610

5

6

*Early Walloon broadsword
c. 1610 side view*

Skeletal form of basket hilt c. 1620
Illustration 7

This is a purely English development of the open-basket hilt for horsemen and cavalry use. The basis of this hilt form is a small number of vertical and horizontal bars connecting a small shallow dish baseguard to a large near spherical pommel. Affording a minimal protection to the hand, it was economical to produce and simplistic in its formation. The vertical layer of bars immediately above the base dish are doubled to give strength to the inner and outer sides of the basket, a feature which has been continued through to the Mortuary sword, of which this form may have been a forerunner. The sword illustrated may have had its origins within the Wolsternholme family at Nostell Priory prior to 1650. The grip has been fashioned from antler horn, smoothed over, then spirally cut, possibly to take a decorative wire, although wire locating points have not been found.

The outer surface of the dish is lightly chiselled with representations of foliage, the whole basket surface being coated with black protective paint. The blade is straight, single edged and tapering into a shallow point, with a narrow fuller at the back-edge. A Running Wolf mark is prominently displayed on an otherwise plain surface.

Blade length	35.38in (89.8cm)
Sword weight	1lb 15oz (0.98kg)

Skeletal form

7

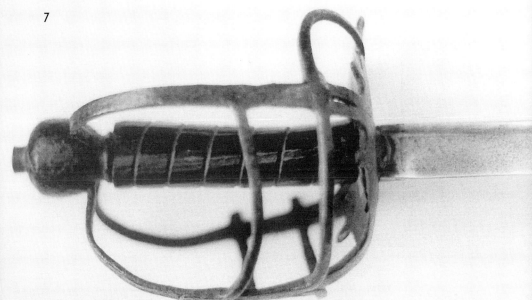

Heavy Walloon Cavalry sword, c. 1620
Illustration 8

This type of sword was prominent in the Thirty Years War principally for cuirassiers of both sides, and adopted or acquired by many of the mercenaries. The hilt is of robust construction with solid circular bars curved vertically and diagonally, and distinguishable by the central 'knoppels' or balusters, forming an open basket from the pommel down to the two solid 'shell' guards. There are a number of variations in the quantity of bars used, but the principle remained that the basket should remain reasonably open. The sword featured has a basket constructed from four curved bars interconnected by only two diagonals.

The base guard is heart shaped; the grip is bound in iron wire with securing iron wire Turks Heads. The blade is elliptical in cross-section with a central fuller. The entire length of the forté is engraved with classical band decoration and stands of arms, and on one side, with a 'crooked' cross, (which may lead one to believe that it belonged to a knight or mounted man-at-arms of one of the Holy Roman Empire Bishoprics: Speier, Worms, Mainz or Treves, nominally part of the Palatinate.)

Blade length	34.13in (86.6cm)
Sword weight	2lb 9oz (1.17kg)

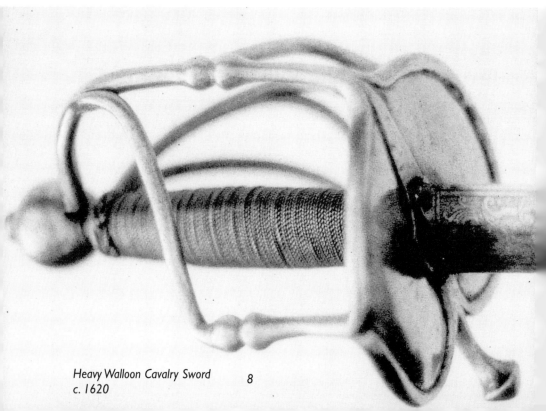

Heavy Walloon Cavalry Sword   8
c. 1620

English Cuirassiers sword from c. 1620
Illustration 9

By comparison to the Walloon cuirassier sword shown in Illustration 8, an English cuirassier sword of the same period and attributed to participation in the Thirty Years War is currently on display at York Castle Museum. This sword, on show with its associated half-armour, has a hilt to a completely different construction from other swords of the period. The basket guard follows the basic shape of a bowl, the outer and inner curved sides cut away as a shaped scallop shell within a circlet and linked on either side to a broad curving knucklebow by a curving bar. The base of the guard terminates in a downward curved quillon. The blade is of flattened elliptical cross-section, centrally fullered, about 36in (91.4cm) in length. This cutaway 'shell' bowl construction could have been a forerunner of the Proto-Mortuary sword.

9

English Cuirassiers sword c. 1620

Open basket hilt of 'Ribbon' construction
Illustration 10

Open basket hilt of 'ribbon' construction

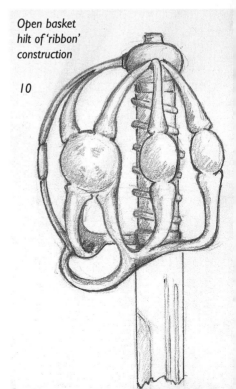

10

This is a direct development from the open basket hilt shown in illustration 4. For this cavalry hilt two influences are apparent, the 'knoppel' effect of the heavy Walloon, but considerably flattened to cater for the 'ribbon' construction adopted in Scottish basket hilts of the period. Good examples of this type of sword have been on display in:

Warwick Castle Armoury (1973)
Littlecote House (1973)

A further example was offered for sale from the Winsbury Collection (1973).

Light Walloon Cavalry sword c. 1630
Illustration 11

The Walloon influence on British Cavalry swords did not stop at the two forms already covered (Illustrations 5, 6 and 8). Out of the Thirty Years War the Walloons developed a much lighter sword, the hilt of which was constructed from a baseguard of two oval 'shells', and the now readily identifiable branched knucklebow connecting the shells to the pommel.

The oval 'shells' could be of varied form: open rings, solid shells, perforated shells, or combinations of these three options. The example shown is that of both shells being perforated. The blade is of broadsword form, marked with a Running Wolf, and tapers to a shallow spear point; there is a small length of central fuller at the forte, decorated with a 'point' pattern.

Blade length   31.37in (79.7cm)
Sword weight 1lb 10oz (0.72kg)

This form of hilt, with small variations, recurs through to the middle of the eighteenth century.

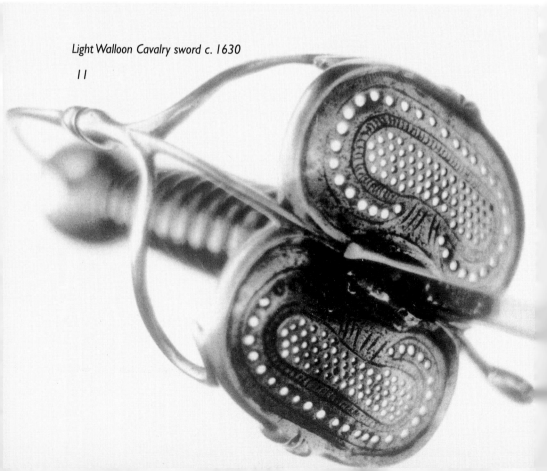

Light Walloon Cavalry sword c. 1630

11

Proto-Mortuary sword
Illustration 12

The term 'proto-mortuary' has only recently been coined to identify the hilt form shown in the illustration, as it was thought to be the forerunner of the Mortuary sword. It is a direct development from the bowl basket guard of the York Castle Museum English cuirassiers sword (Illustration 9) but also has the Walloon influence of the branched knucklebow, and it was a sword subject to several 'patterns' in Fairfax's New Model Army. In the example shown, the three guard extensions are shaped, and chiselled with striations in the form of scallop shells, and typical of the form for many of these swords. The grip is of polished burred wood and is another noticeable utilization of natural materials of the British environment and landscape by British craftsmen.

The blade is of single-edged backsword type with a fuller towards the back edge. There are no armourer's marks or decoration to the blade.

Blade length (shortened)	31in (81.25cm)
Sword weight	2lb 7oz (1.1kg)

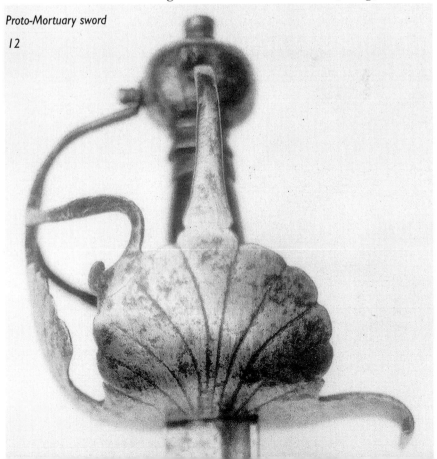

Proto-Mortuary sword

12

The Mortuary sword
Illustrations 13, 14 and 15

The Mortuary sword has received a lot of publicity as a weapon used throughout the Civil War by both sides of the conflict. Deservedly so, as it is peculiar to British weaponry and carried mainly by the officers and gentlemen of the cavalry units, generally recognizable by the formation of the hilt and the mask decoration applied to the surface of the baseguard. The general formation of the mortuary hilt is that of a dished baseguard connected to the pommel by a branched knucklebow and two side branches, generally stiffened by double branches towards the baseguard.

Added to this structure there then may be additional branches from the knucklebow branch. One can therefore readily recognize the mortuary origins from the skeletal form, Walloon and proto-mortuary swords already shown. For the example illustrated, the baseguard surface decoration is that typically of four masks, but interspersed in the diagonal sections are raised representations of strange fish-like creatures (dolphins). The basket is built up above the dish by the standard branched knucklebow, with one paired set of bars parallel with the knucklebow branch, and a further set of curved bars at the rear of the guard. The blade is a double-edged broadsword with a limited central fuller in which are the residual marks of 'INIMINI'. At the end of the fuller are the marks of a Cross and a Running Wolf.

Blade length	33.87in (86cm)
Sword weight	2lb 5oz (1.05kg)

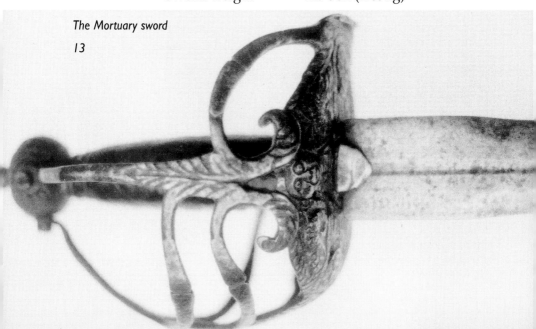

The Mortuary sword

13

14

The Mortuary sword

Sample range of Mortuary sword guard decorations that one is likely to encounter

15

Troopers' swords during this period did not differ substantially in principle from the form of their officers' swords, only in terms of simplicity and economy of construction, as shown in illustration 16.

Troopers' swords of this period   16

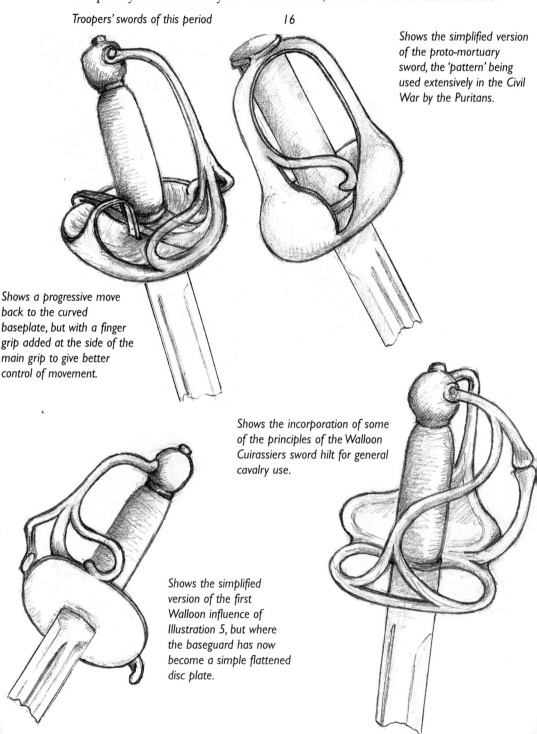

Shows the simplified version of the proto-mortuary sword, the 'pattern' being used extensively in the Civil War by the Puritans.

Shows a progressive move back to the curved baseplate, but with a finger grip added at the side of the main grip to give better control of movement.

Shows the incorporation of some of the principles of the Walloon Cuirassiers sword hilt for general cavalry use.

Shows the simplified version of the first Walloon influence of Illustration 5, but where the baseguard has now become a simple flattened disc plate.

Life Guards' sword, 1660-1688
Illustrations 17 and 18

In 1971 the Household Cavalry Museum displayed a light Walloon cavalry sword with gilt brass furnishings bearing a particular design cast in relief on the shell guards as Exhibit 8, with the title 'Sword of a Private Gentleman of the Lifeguard – 1660-1688'. That sword, apart from having a Solingen blade, was identical to that now portrayed in this history. The allegorical story attached to the swords of this relief design is that on his accession to the throne, Charles II gathered his courtiers and friends about him and, being both short of money and still fearful for his security, offered them a favoured position as private gentlemen troopers in his Lifeguard for a particular sum of money. There was no shortage of takers to this proposition.

In becoming members of this exclusive 'club', these gentlemen adopted a standard form of sword hilt, that form being the favoured light Walloon with solid shell guards and branched knucklebow which was suitable for both cavalry action and also as a court sword. Whilst the blades of these swords may not have been identical in make or length, the cast-in relief to the shell guards was identical. The illustrations show the general form of the sword, and the detail of the relief design: a central crowned lions head, about which are dispersed a lion and a unicorn, an angel, and a representation of an oak tree in front of which a man stands with a

Life Guards' sword, 1660-1688 relief design

17

long devils tail. This could be interpreted in a cynical way: the oak tree representing the blasted oak in which Charles II sheltered at Boscobel after the Battle of Worcester and the angel who delivered him from the searching Parliamentarians (devils), and allowed him to take his rightful place on the throne of England. It is noteworthy that oak leaves and acorns recur as decorations on some cavalry swords at later dates, particularly for those regiments that may have been formed, such as the Life Guards, following the Restoration.

Life Guards sword, 1660-1688

18

The sword illustrated has the standard Walloon hilt formation of double shell guards, large spherical pommel and branched recurring knucklebow, all in brass. The relief design is on both inner and outer surfaces of the shell guards, and either side of the pommel. There is also a mask cast into the centre of the knucklebow, which may be in remembrance of Charles I. The blade is of Dutch manufacture, broadsword in form, tapering, and with a central fuller in which the name of the armourer is etched: 'Willem Hor'. The armourer's mark of a crucifix follows at the end of the fuller. The grip is heavily roped in brass wire, and secured in position by brass wire Turks Heads.

Blade length	30.87in (70.85cm)
Sword weight	1lb 14oz (0.85kg)

That this relief design was the first to be adopted by a regiment, albeit gentlemen and nobility in its entirety, was an obvious honour and determined to be recognized as such. This honour was never repeated, until Regimental Battle Honours were recorded on British Cavalry swords from the late eighteenth century.

This was not the only case of the eventual Household Cavalry adopting the light Walloon sword. The Household Cavalry Museum also displayed Exhibit 9, listed as 'Officers Sword of the Royal Horse Guards, 1661.' The officer in fact was Aubrey de Vere, Earl of Oxford, First Colonel of the Royal Horse Guards. The brass shell guards portray in relief a boars head within a garter (the de Vere family crest). The blade has a Running Wolf mark. This sword also has an interesting story in that it became lost, to be recovered much later from a barn in Hungerford, and was eventually acquired by Baroness Burdett Coutts, who had it refurbished, gilt and blued, and presented to Henry Irving as an appreciation of his acting ability.

Multibar basket hilt c. 1681

Following the accession of Charles II the development of the cavalry sword hilt became more expansive to match the settling down of the country. This typical example is the transformation of the light Walloon sword into a fully fledged open basket hilt by the simple addition of a number of curved bars either side of the grip. The example shown has three curved bars added to the outer side, and two to the inner side. The fixing of these bars to the solid shell guards was always a delicate operation in brass, the differential stresses in the opposing masses often creating breaks and cracks at the join when the materials 'settled'. This is the case in this particular sword where one of the inside bars has broken away.

The grip is of rectangular cross-section wood bearing the imprint of a heavy roped wire. The wire Turks Heads however are still in position. The blade has been cut-down from a back-edge three fullered rapier blade bearing the etching 'Andrea Ferara'.

Blade length	31.75in (81.7cm)
Sword weight	1lb 14oz (0.85kg)

Multibar basket hilt c. 1681

19

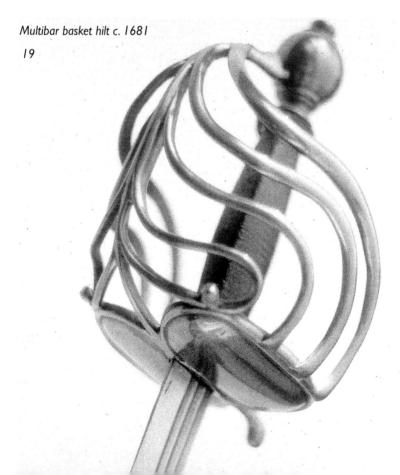

CHAPTER 3

1700 – 1780

The turn of the century found Britain in an expansive mood, the puritan regimes incurred from the Civil War had been relaxed, and the new royalty move was both to the liking of the politicians and the people, giving an air of impetus and confidence to undertake new ventures, exploration, to colonize ever more distant lands and extend its trade throughout the known world. The expansion of these activities meant protection of the trading routes and protection of the new colonies, inevitably extending the scope of naval and army operations. However, the new Dutch, and later the new Hanoverian royalties brought about new alliances in Europe and the precipitation of the British into new wars in Europe:

- 1701-14 The War of the Spanish Succession, most notable by the defeat of the French by the British at Blenheim.
- 1718-20 The War of the Quadruple Alliance.
- 1740-48 The War of the Austrian Succession.
- 1756-63 The Seven Years War, where Britain secured Canada from the French.

And, not withstanding the Act of Union of 1707 whereby Scotland ceded into Great Britain, the putting down of two Jacobite rebellions in 1715 and 1745. This near continuous state of war and armed conflict, not always successful from the British point of view, but giving some significant victories over the French from time to time, often showed that European allies were inconsistent in their allegiances to each other and were motivated only by their own concerns or political gains and not necessarily by the needs of the temporarily united countries. Moreover, it demanded a larger standing army and naval concentration that was conversant with the changing tactics and strategy of European warfare. The cavalry had to adapt to the differences in terrain and the use of lightly armed horseborne skirmishers that were now common in Austria and the German states. The need to improve and increase arms was met early in the century by the establishment of Boards of Ordnance whose objectives were to ensure that all arms were consistent in quality of manufacture and passed a few set standard inspections and tests to demonstrate fitness for purpose, conditions which had first been initiated by the Parliamentarians in the Civil War but which had become somewhat relaxed. This expansive period was also reflected in the form of the arms, particularly for the cavalry where the sword hilt became noticeably more flamboyant and ostentatious, and more protective to the hand, reverting to the full baskets in many instances. These sword hilts, whilst reflecting the Scottish influences of their basket hilts, were now becoming uniquely British. Without becoming 'standard patterns' in the heavier cavalry units, they were becoming more recognizable as belonging to the cavalry, and to some particular regiments. During this period, it was the prerogative of the regiment's colonel to define the mode of dress and the arms to be used. Then, in the last quarter of the century Britain met its first real humiliating defeat at the hands of its own American colonists in the War of American Independence (1775-1783), a war that Britain was not logistically prepared for, and did not understand, either the psychology or the determination or the motivational instincts by which these hardened colonists were able to conduct their own distinctive military campaigns.

The sword hilts illustrated in this section can only be representative of the diversity encountered in this period of cavalry sword history and Britain's period of expansion.

Anglicized Walloon hilt c. 1700-1740
Illustration 20

At the beginning of the century the Walloon branched knucklebow had become an identifiable and constant feature of the British Cavalry sword. The illustration shows a further anglicization in which the branched side-scrolls have been deleted. The hilt furniture is brass, the double shell guards are solid and plain, and there is a minimum of decoration to the knucklebow; the grip is totally bound in roped brass wire, and contained by brass wire Turks Heads. The blade is of broadsword form, with heavy lenticular section, tapering to a spear point. The central fuller is etched with 'INIMINI', and stamped with a Board of Ordnance viewing mark of a crown over arrow; residual Running Wolf marks are present. (An interesting stamped number is also present on one side, '14482920', reminiscent of the eight figure British Army personnel numbers in existence towards the end and immediately after the Second World War).

This particular form of cavalry sword would have been typical of both officers and other ranks at the time of the War of the Spanish Succession.

Blade length	30.88in (78.5cm)
Sword weight	2lbs (0.9kg)

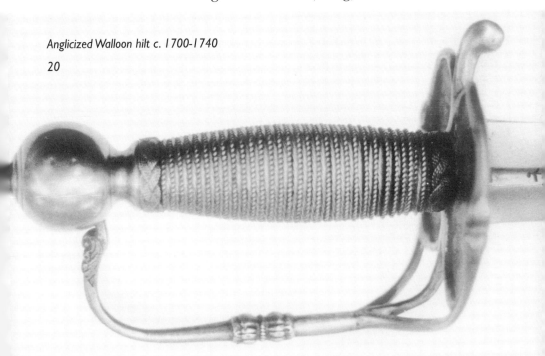

Anglicized Walloon hilt c. 1700-1740

20

Horse Grenadier Guards 1740-50
Illustration 21

Attributions of sword hilt form is always difficult to attain and substantiate, but the hilt illustrated has been attributed to an officer of the Horse Grenadier Guards before 1760, possibly of the 2nd Scots Troop. This attribution is based on the writhen curved bars and the presence of the acorn finials, (refer to Chapter 2, illustrations 17 and 18), and oil paintings of the period. This particular sword has two further distinguishing features: a broad knucklebow built up from four formed bars with a central acorn finial and a baseguard of rudimentary open honeysuckle scrolls; (a motif which will be found to recur as a standard feature on the later pattern cavalry swords). The grip is covered in sharkskin, but with no binding wire, although there is a spiral depression to accommodate one if desired. One residual Turks Head is still present, as is the circular leather liner over the baseguard. The blade is straight, single edged and broad fullered with a false-edge over the last 9in to a spear point.

Some blade etching remains residual as 'SOL———', a cockerel armourer's mark is present at the forté, which may indicate the blade to have been an early manufacture of Gebrüder Weyersberg.

Blade length	34in (86.5cm)
Sword weight	1lb 15oz (0.88kg)

Horse Grenadier Guards officer c. 1740-50

21

Horse Grenadier Troopers' sword c.1740-1760
Illustration 22

The principle behind a plain 4-bar hilt, with some variations, became the basic form of the troopers' sword for the Horse Grenadier Guards from about 1740. The 4-bar hilt form with writhen bars and swirled pommel was adopted by some Horse Grenadier Guard officers, and other cavalry officers from about 1760 through to 1780. For the Troopers sword as shown the 4-bar guard forms a half-basket on the outer side between the knucklebow and the double heart shaped open base-guard; the grip is fish-skin covered, secured by metal ferrules below a spherical pommel. The blade is of broadsword form, with a $7^1/4$ in central fuller, tapering to a spear point. There are no armourers' marks or other means of identification.

Blade length	32in (82cm)
Sword weight	1lb 11oz (0.73kg)

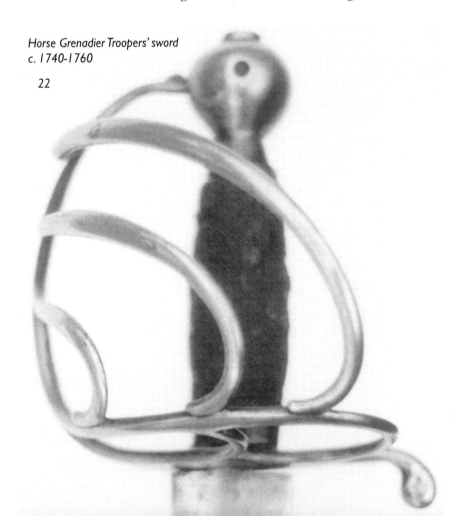

Horse Grenadier Troopers' sword
c. 1740-1760

22

Dual purpose c. 1750-1775
Illustration 23

In all probability the sword of the hilt illustrated would have served the dual purpose of both service and dress. With hilt furniture in brass of two outer curved bars and one inner curved bar branching from the knucklebow, and open heart shaped baseguard, the half basket gives a minimum hand protection about the fish-skin and copper wire bound grip secured in position by an urn-shaped pommel, which would have been typical of the period. The blade is only one inch wide, single edged, broad fullered and tapering to a shallow spear point, profusely decorated over 12in of its length:

i. A Stand of Arms; scrolled foliage; an early form of Britannia standing by an anchor; a wigged mask; various forms of foliage.

ii. A Stand of Arms with a Union Jack; a Stand of Arms supporting a mop capped figure of hope; an urn midst foliage with an acorn finial sprouting more foliage (refer to text for illustrations 17 and 18) possibly representing the rejuvenation of the country following the restoration of 1661).

Blade length	31³/₄in (80.7cm)
Sword weight	1lb 9oz (0.7kg)

Dual purpose c. 1750-1775

23

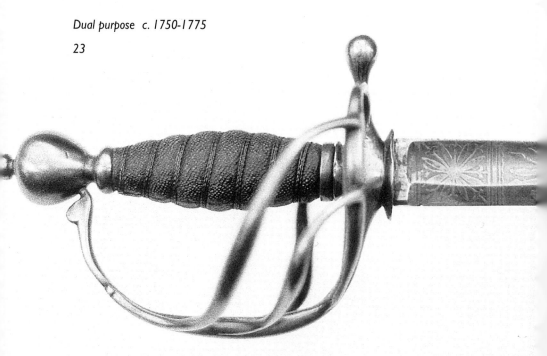

Stand of Arms hilt
Illustration 24

This hilt form is uniquely British and known to have been used by a number of Dragoon Regiments, in the plain form for troopers, and with the Stand of Arms decorations for officers. The background history which has established this form is interesting.

Charles Ffoulkes and Hopkinson appear to be the first to have brought this hilt form into public notice by their book *Sword, Lance and Bayonet* published in 1938 through to 1967, and subsequently by Ffoulkes in *Arms and Armament*, 1945 – 47, in which Illustration 32 shows a Dragoon sword hilt of 1742. This is a simple drawing with no perspective, of what appears to be a bowl hilt with four recurving apertures, and thought to be a troopers sword of the 1st Royal Dragoons. It was Ffoulkes' opinion that no examples of this hilt form existed and that none ever would.

However, further substantive evidence of the presence of this troopers' form of cavalry sword, as sketched by Ffoulkes, has lately been gained from the reading of a *Regimental history of the 7th Own Queens Hussars (7th Light Dragoons)* by C.R.B. Barrett and published in two volumes in 1914. This book is notable in that it has a complete chapter devoted to the weapons used by the 7th Light Dragoons/Hussars, and shows eleven sketches of swords and other weapons, ranging from one similar to Illustration 4 to the regulation pattern troopers' sword of 1908. Barrett's sketch 3 is of particular interest in that it shows the same hilt presented by Ffoulkes with 'four curious twisted single barred piercings' as represented in the Duke of Cumberland's book (which was, presumably, a means of defining dress regulations at that time). Further, this type of sword was determined to be the official sword for Dragoons in 1742.

The lack of perspective in the sketch has shown only one set of apertures. In reality the actual bowl guard is formed by three curved plates separated by two sets of four apertures. In *Swords and Blades of the American Revolution*, 1973, Neumann shows ref: 268.S. as being an English Horseman's sabre, c. 1750, (i.e. for a trooper), in which small recurring bars actually define the shape of the apertures. Since that date one example has come up for sale through Wallis & Wallis Sale 346 on 14 March 1990. This has a plain undecorated hilt, and was considered to be the Troopers' version of this form.

Four views of the Stand of Arms hilt

24

The officers' version (decorated) was specifically noted by A.V.B. Norman in an article *The Dating and Identification of some Swords in the Royal Collection at Windsor Castle*, which appeared in the *Arms and Armour Journal* Volume IX, No. 6, December 1979, Plate LXXI.B. In this example the three curved plates are not as wide as for the troopers' sword, and the recurving bars are longer. The three guard plates are decorated with chiselled trophies and stand of arms, the outer surfaces being polished bright, and the inner surface lined with white leather. The blade is a multi-fullered back-sword 32 $^9/_{16}$ in long. The origins of this sword were listed as 'Scotch', and it was manufactured by Bland of London. Norman has attributed this sword to between 1768 and 1788, and to particular Dragoon regiments, those later becoming the 1st Royals, 5th and 7th Dragoons with steel fittings, and the 3rd Dragoons in brass; there is no attribution for those regiments that later became Dragoon Guards, although he has quoted a portrait of 1749 of a colonel of the 1st Troop Horse Grenadier Guards as carrying an example of this sword. Norman further notes that, apart from the example in Windsor Castle, at that time, one example was in the Hermitage Museum, Leningrad, and two examples were known to be in private collections.

It is not known, however, if the illustrated example is one of the latter. Probably not. The detail shown in the illustrations and following text will give a more explicit understanding of this unique form of British cavalry steel sword hilt:

Inner panel is an open scroll of honeysuckle fronds. Knuckleguard panel is chiselled with a Stand of Arms containing a helmet and flags. The outer panel is chiselled with a Stand of Arms containing a drum and flags. The baseguard is an open scroll of honeysuckle fronds. The guard is finished with a sheet quillon in crown form, typical of cavalry swords of that period. The cream coloured sharkskin grip is bound with copper wire and secured in position by top and bottom ferrules. The hemispherical pommel is also distinctive in that it is cut with curved triangular depressions. The blade is broadsword in form, lenticular in cross-section, tapering with a central fuller. There are no manufacturing or armourers' marks.

Blade length	32in (82.8cm)
Sword weight	2lb (0.9kg)

American War of Independence

The twenty-five years preceding the American War of Independence were truly those which showed the expansive mood of the country and the versatility of the design and form of the cavalry sword hilt. There is little retained in British records about which type of sword was used by which regiment at the approach of the War of American Independence, but Neumann in his two books, (which include a number of British Cavalry swords of pre-Revolutionary vintage), gives a very good account of all the swords that would or could have been used by, or were available to the American colonists. These swords originated from Britain, Germany, France and Holland from as far back as 1635 through to 1780. Again, there is no attempt to account for regiments; how America came by these swords can be explained away in general terms.

During the colonization of the Americas weapons of all kinds and ages were taken into the country by the colonists for their own protection. As the colony enlarged and prospered, new arms were imported from Europe and Britain, either for personal use, or to arm the local militia units being formed for local protection. The eventual establishment of military arsenals of arms that had previously been standard weapons in the British Army, were intended for the army units drafted in from Britain to assist local Governors and the Governor General to maintain law and order (and the resultant capture of some of those arsenals by the insurgents). These would be logical reasons in a new and developing country, consequently at the time and during the insurrection there would have been a broad range of weapons, of different time periods, available to the colonists with which to wage war. Not withstanding these reasons, the colonists also established many local manufacturers that were capable of producing adequate arms to supplement an ever growing arsenal.

Thus the sources of arms to the American revolutionists were many and they used what they could and how they could to their advantage. The tragedy here is that during a period of British expansion, and at a time when the cavalry sword hilt was at times quite spectacular (and Neumann would be the first to acknowledge that during this period they were 'innovative') there are precious few examples remaining in Britain for reference. Perhaps they are all in the United States of America.

In the main, the British swords shown by Neumann would be termed 'heavy' cavalry swords. Ffoulkes and Norman have attributed one of the swords, Neumann 268.5, to the 1st Dragoons and other heavy Dragoon regiments, but none of these served in America. Only two British cavalry regiments served in the American War of Independence, namely the 16th and 17th Light Dragoons, whose swords are rather indeterminate for that period due to a lack of records. There is one document that could indicate it to be of the form shown in Illustration 31, or possibly an earlier version of Illustration 33, or Neumann 134.5 and 144.5. The only heavy cavalry that Great Britain were known to use were those mercenaries from Germany, principally of Brunswick and Hesse, who willingly contracted to supply complete regiments to fight in America. It is recorded that the Brunswick Dragoons surrendered at the Battle of Bennington, and that their swords were acquired by Washington to equip a newly raised American Regiment. Those swords, however, are believed to be similar to Illustration 4 and Neumann 247.5. Other possibilities would be that various forms were intended for the British Legion horse regiments raised by Banastre Tarleton, that stalwart loyalist cavalryman whose devestating actions were decried by the rebels, but who also brought into existence the Tarleton Helmet for the British Cavalry.

A selection of the swords of this particular period follows.

Scallop Shell Guard c. 1750 – 1780
Illustration 25

The sword illustrated shows the departure from the simple Walloon form to one of the more flamboyant styles being adopted from the middle of the century. This scallop shell form, although a consistent motif in Britain in the seventeenth century was also being adopted for cavalry swords in many of the European states. It was a form that gave both adequate protection and a purpose of display. The sword shown has brass furnishings, the main shell guard supported from a narrow base with small inner shell, and connected to the knucklebow by three curved bars. The pommel is spherical, retaining the guard and grip, which is leather covered and spirally bound with thick brass wire. The blade is single-edged, tapering to a 7in false edge

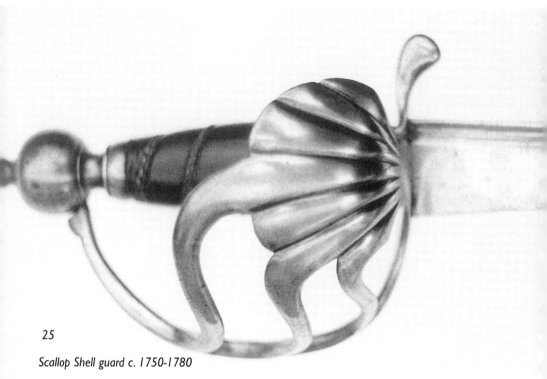

25

Scallop Shell guard c. 1750-1780

shallow spear point. The blade is not decorated but has a Running Fox and the initials 'S.H' on each side, indicating the manufacturer to be from the Harvey family (three of the name Samuel) operating from addresses in London between 1748 and 1800.

Blade length	33in (84.8cm)
Sword weight	2lb (0.9kg)

Neumann also shows the Running Fox/S.H. mark in his works and a number of Scallop guard cavalry swords of European origin:

253.5-English 1650-1680 Blade Length 32.75in Proto-Mortuary form.

293.5-German 1750-1765 Blade Length 33.38in Pommel combined with backstrap and thumb ring present. 2 curved bars.

294.5-German 1765-1780 Blade Length 31in Sim. 3 curved bars.

299.5-French 1750-1770 Blade 34in Solid heart baseguard.

300.5-French 1750-1765 Blade 35.75in Sim to 253.5.

4-Bar hilt form c. 1720-1780
Illustration 26

This hilt form is recognizable as being consistent with British Dragoon swords during this period, with the Bar hilt form becoming the basis of the standard cavalry patterns during the nineteenth Century. The sword as illustrated has steel furniture of an urn pommel retaining a basket guard of knucklebow with three re-curving outer and two re-curving inner bars, above an open double heart shaped base. The grip is fishskin covered, bound in copper wire. The blade is of a light falchion curved form (forerunner of the 1796 pattern Light Cavalry sabre), with single edge and 3 narrow fullers at the back edge. The blade was intended to be plain, but has a residual etching 6in from the forté on the outer side but which is not recognizably British, that of head and shoulders of a mature woman.

The residual wording above the etching is unfortunately not readily decipherable but may be shown as '.A..D...ER'. In all probability this could be one of the swords that changed hands during the war but has come back into British hands at a later date.

Blade length	33.13in (84.2cm)
Sword weight	2lb 3oz (0.98kg)

Other similar examples have been noted in Britain: Warwick Castle, 1973.

(i) Identical Falchion form with an Arabic inscription;
(ii) Backsword blade; rein-ring built into basket.

Neumann records similar, but not identical swords:

127.5-English 1720-40 3 Bars either side; back-edge blade, 29.75in
128.5-English 1740-60 3 Bars either side; back-edge blade, 32.25in
132.5-English 1770-80 3 bars outer side only; broadsword blade 31.63in

Scallop Shell guard c. 1750-1780

26

Scottish open S-hilt c. 1760-80
Illustration 27

Again, this hilt form is British, reflecting many aspects of Scottish basket hilt features and influences, with the open bar work in brass, the principle recognition feature being the 'S' bar between separating vertical bars, two on the outer side, one on the inner, and the open base being of heart-shape extending into a broad crown quillon. The flattened urn pommel secures the basket about a fishskin covered grip spirally bound in brass wire, with top and bottom brass wire Turks Heads. The blade is of flattened triangular cross section, slightly tapered to a spear point and marked with a Board of Ordnance crown above 'GR/IEF/RIS', that is, manufactured by Jefferies (sometimes Jeffrey's) of London, probably within the limits 1763 to 1777.

Blade length	35.75in (90.8cm)
Sword weight	2lb 15oz (1.34kg)

The sword illustrated is representative of the Troopers' usage. Officers' swords were very similar, but generally the blade was decorated; two officers' swords have recently come up for sale:

i. Wallis & Wallis Sale of 1999, with double edged blade, 35in long, etched with foliage and scrollwork, and the motto: 'RECTE FACIENDO NEMINEM LIMENS'

ii. Wallis & Wallis Sale 381, 1994, with 28 $^1/_2$" 'wavy' blade.

Neumann gives only one example of a Troopers' Sword:

272.5-English Horseman's Saber, c. 1750, German Blade, British Board of Ordnance mark, 34in long.

Note: In the lately discovered Regimental History of the 7th Queens Own Hussars (7th Light Dragoons), referred to in the introduction of page 43, this type of sword is stated to have been used by that regiment, but at a date no later than 1714.

Scottish open S-hilt c.1710-80

27

Honeysuckle basket hilt c. 1760-80
Illustration 28

Hitherto the honeysuckle has been portrayed in a limited form only on British cavalry swords, but the abundance with which the honeysuckle grew and flowered in British hedgerows was not to be ignored, in fact almost, after the rose, a British emblem. It was only a matter of time before it would be adopted as a decoration for swords, in particular cavalry swords, and this occurred in the middle of the eighteenth century. The illustration shows such a sword of a Dragoon officer, where the entire three -quarter basket is cut out with bands of honeysuckle scrolling. The securing pommel is a striated urn, the grip, originally of wood, has been reinforced and re-covered with black leather and spirally bound with brass wire. The original shaped leather liner is still present. The blade is straight, broad fullered and single edged, tapering to a spear point.

Blade length	34.25in (87cm)
Sword weight	1lb 15oz (0.9kg)

The honeysuckle theme will be found to recur on British Cavalry swords in the early nineteenth century on all officers cavalry swords as standard patterns through to the early Twentieth Century.

Neumann records one similar example:

147.5-English Short Saber, 1780-1790, with a more open form of honeysuckle; blade is a Hounslow backsword type, 31.63in long.

Honeysuckle basket hilt c. 1760-80

28

Triangular frontal guard c. 1740-1780
Illustration 29

This relatively simple basket surround appears to be the first and only instance of it being used by British Cavalry. The form is instantly recognizable, the usual knucklebow having been extended into a broad triangular frontal plate at right angles to a dished circular base plate, the two connected by curved bars running parallel to the frontal plate. The pommel is conical, the grip of black covering leather spirally bound with iron wire. The blade is straight, tapered, single edged and bi-fullered.

Blade length	35.38in (89.8cm)
Sword weight	2lb 10oz (1.2kg)

Neumann records a similar example:

266.5-English Horseman's Saber c. 1755, bi-fullered blade marked 'Harvey', 35.13in long

A number of examples have come up in British sales in recent years:

i. Kent Arms Sales, 1975, flat pommel, tapering single fullered blade 35in long, c. 1740.

ii. Wallis & Wallis Sale 234, 1977, tapering single edged bi-fullered blade, 34in long, c. 1755.

iii. Wallis & Wallis Sale 254, 1980, straight single edged bi-fullered blade, 35in long, c. 1760.

iv. Wallis & Wallis Sale 294, 1984, Urn pommel, tapering blade, narrow fuller at back edge, 28^1/4in long, c. 1750.

v. Wallis & Wallis Sale 300, 1985, hemispherical pommel, tapering single fullered blade, 33in long, c.1755.

vi. A sword of similar form, but with the triangular side extensions replaced with two diagonal bars in the Walloon style came up through the sales in 1972 and was identified as that of a mid eighteenth century Canadian Dragoon Broadsword, and authenticated by the *Canadian Journal of Arms Collecting*.

Triangular frontal guard
c. 1740-1780

29

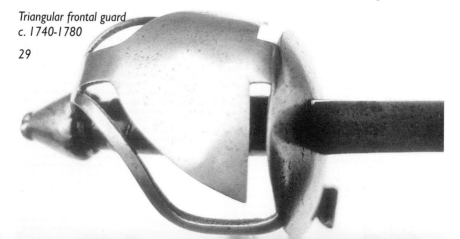

Innovative hilt design c. 1750-1770
Illustration 30

This is the form of cavalry hilt that Neumann refers to as innovative, in which the three-quarter basket guard utilizes architectural arch design, representations of shells, and even fish (possibly salmon), and eels as the bars of the basket. If the fish is a salmon then it is possible that the dragoon regiment, whose officers used these swords, was Scottish. The example illustrated is of a full three-quarter basket; a variant is in existence where the guard is interrupted by a large side rein-ring. The grip is covered in sharkskin, spirally bound with copper wire and trimmed with copper wire Turks Heads. The blade is lenticular in cross-section, tapering, with two small fullers either side of the armourer's marks, 'ANDREA' on one side, 'FARARA' on the other, each two letters being interspersed with an impressed turbanned head.

Blade length	35.75in (90.8cm)
Sword weight	2lb 6oz (1.08kg)

Neumann's example has the included rein-ring, and a multi fullered blade by 'ANDRIA FERARA', 33.25in long. Frederick Wilkinson also illustrates the rein-ring form in *Swords and Daggers*. The blade is of broad-fullered backsword form, 38.5in long. A further rein-ring version came up for sale in Wallis & Wallis Connoisseurs' Sale of 7 October 1998, the blade of bi-fullered backsword form, 34.75in long.

Innovative hilt design c. 1750-1770

30

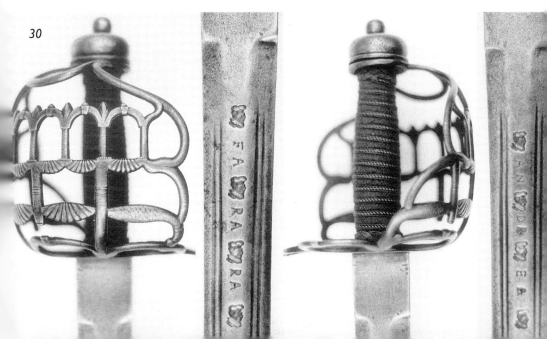

During this period, Light Dragoons were instituted into the British Cavalry. This strategical change in British Military thinking was not initially directed at North American warfare but principally at European. It was an adaptation to terrain that was ever changing from open to wooded, and where speed was essential in both action and reconnaissance and the relaying of intelligence back to those in command, becoming an ever demanding necessity. The weaponry was correspondingly lighter than that used by existing Dragoons who had always tended to heavier armament, although there was no immediate attempt to follow the lines of the Sinclair Sabel (Illustration 2) developed towards the end of the seventeenth century, the guard of which now might be termed cumbersome. In practice the light cavalry sword from 1750 through to about 1770 was applied to only a few regiments and was an even simpler affair, constructed from a grip with pommel, simple cross guard, and a slightly curved fullered blade. A.V.B Norman notes two good examples of such a form in his article on the Windsor Castle collection, both of the 15th Light Dragoons and typical of the earlier lighter swords of this period. It was not until the 1780's that a stirrup hilt or knucklebow was added to the hilt. The second development significant to this period was one of dress regulations whereby officers and men were to use the same swords. Whilst the principle of this was observed in many cavalry regiments, there was considerable licence applied by the officers to differentiate themselves from their men, but apart from these anomalies we have the beginnings of standardization. The light cavalry swords are described in Chapter 4.

Chapter 4

LIGHT CAVALRY 1760 – 1796

By 1780 the Light Dragoons were reasonably established as a fighting arm within the British Army, and soon became known as the Light Cavalry. Their swords were initially of a varied nature and differing considerably from the heavier and basket hiltedforms covered in Chapter 3 in that the basket hilt was dispensed with and replaced with a simple cross hilt similar to that shown in Illustration 31. Such a sword was in use with the 15th Light Dragoons between 1764 and 1788. The more common alternative to this form was a sword with a simple knucklebow bar to give a limited protection to the hand; these designs were intended to decrease the weight of the sword and the fatigue of the user.

It was not until about 1780 that the dress regulations and Board of Ordnance recognized that their swords should be of more substantial construction, and in keeping with the forms coming out of Eastern Europe, which were fast being adopted by the central and western European military nations. From that date a number of changes were made to arrive at the first standards for weapons for use by cavalry and other fighting arms. The object of these standards, or patterns as they later became known, was to initially devise a weapon that would withstand the worst effects in fighting, and to serve the purpose of that particular arm within the limits of manufacture and basic testing.

Once the Board of Ordnance were satisfied that a form was suitable, a number of Patterns would be made and lodged at some convenient armoury or manufactory so that selected manufacturers or suppliers could view their construction and discuss the 'specification' before bidding for quantity manufacture, as required by the Board of Ordnance. This procedure did not necessarily produce standard weapons in every respect; invariably there were minor variations due to manufacturing techniques or due to interpretation of the specification. Swords produced by one contractor did not

Simple light cavalry sword c. 1750-1775

31

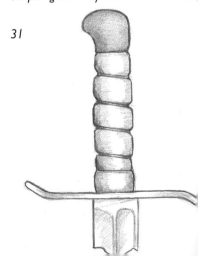

always look the same as those produced by another, and blades were still being imported from abroad to be hilted in Britain, causing further variations. Nevertheless, standard patterns were developing, and from 1788 standard regulation patterns were issued for cavalry swords. Examples leading into and including the 1788 and 1796 Light Cavalry regulation patterns are shown through Illustrations 32 to 52 inclusive.

The Tower of London (1972) c. 1780 had three light cavalry swords on exhibition which clearly showed the immediate changes from simple cross hilt sword to one of more robust construction but light enough for dragoon use.

Light Cavalry sword c.1780   Illustration 32

This is the recognisable form of the 1780 light cavalry sword with hilt furniture in brass, the grip of formed wood covered in fish skin, but devoid of binding wire, retained over the blade tang by a combined 'helmet' pommel and backstrap anchored into a

Light Cavalry sword c.1780

32

lower ferrule; the knucklebow or 'D' shaped stirrup guard extends into a narrow base guard with two downward pointing langets over the blade forté, and into a long rear quillon. The blade of the sword illustrated is straight, single edged and of a wedge cross section, with clipped point, one side stamped with a crown over I. (i.e. the blade, probably of British manufacture, had been inspected and found to be satisfactory by the Board of Ordnance.)

As a fighting sword, this particular form is unwieldy, and its cutting action may have been put in doubt, and may have been better employed in riots, using the flat of the blade. The centre of balance is about 8in from the

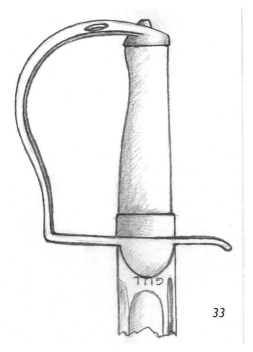

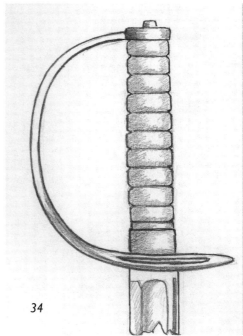

Tower c. 1780-1790 type 1   *Tower c. 1780-1790 type 2*

guard; if the blade had been fullered to move the balance to about 5in from the guard, then the cutting action and handleability of the sword would have been vastly improved.

Blade length	Sword weight
36in (91.5cm)	2lb 5oz (1.15kg)

Tower c. 1780-1790   illustration 33 type 1

For this sword the pommel, stirrup guard (with sword knot aperture), base guard, langet and quillon were an integral structure. The blade was straight, single edged, bi-fullered and spear pointed, and was stamped 'Gill' at the forté. For the dates given Thomas Gill was a sword manufacture operating out of Birmingham.

Tower c. 1780-1790   illustration 34 type 2

Two examples of this form were exhibited with curved knucklebows and slotted basguards (a feature that would be repeated in the 1788 Heavy Cavalry patterns). The blades were straight, single edged and bi-fullered, one having a spear point, the second with a hatchet point.

1788 Pattern Light Cavalry sword

Both officers and men carried the same form of sabre, the blade for men being plain, the blades for officers generally carrying some form of decoration.

Imported, dated 1789
Illustration 34

An officers' sword clearly showing the recognition feature of the 1788 Light Cavalry sabre of the combined helmet pommel and backstrap extension, the upper pommel plate projecting out over the knucklebow juncture. The grip is covered in sharkskin, with grooves to take a binding wire if required. The blade is single edged, with both broad and narrow fullers, and unlike the four preceding swords, is curved with a spear point. The back edge has a deep etching: 'R (for Runkel) Solingen 1789'. Both sides of the blade are decorated with 'Vivat Hussar' above a horseman with cloak and plumed Middle Eastern style helmet, brandishing a scimitar. This is an example of an imported blade, decorated in the east European manner, and subsequently hilted in Britain to meet the requirements of the 1788 pattern.

Blade length
35.63in (90.5cm)

Sword weight
1lb 10 oz (0.75kg)

34

*Light cavalry
sword 1789*

British Light Cavalry, 1788 Pattern
Illustration 36i and ii

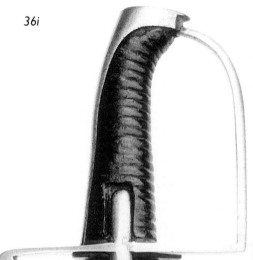

36i

This is the more readily recognizable form of the 1788 pattern Light Cavalry Sabre hilt, still utilizing the flat projecting pommel plate, but now employing double langets from the base guard. The sword portrayed is that of an officer, but the ribbed grip is covered in leather. The blade is curved with broad and narrow fullers, bears no manufacturer's

Typical decoration for 1788 pattern.

36ii

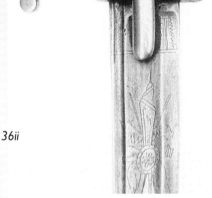

British Light Cavalry, 1788 pattern.

marks, and has been damaged in its working life, repaired and shortened.

The decoration is relatively simplistic:
 i) A Stand of Arms with cavalry helmet, GR and crown
 ii) Urn with flames, mask, foliage and flowers.

Blade length
33.25in (84.5cm)
Sword weight
1lb 14 oz (0.88kg)

Adjustable second knucklebow
Illustration 37

This shows a variation to the standard form of hilt in that an adjustable second knucklebow has been added inside the static knucklebow to give further protection to the hand. In this instance double langets have been added onto the baseguard. This sword has been refurbished at some time with a new wooden grip. There are no signs of residual decoration to the blade, which is bi-fullered and has a shallow hatchet point.

Blade length	33.1in (84cm)
Sword weight	1lb 11oz (0.75kg)

Adjustable second knucklebow

37

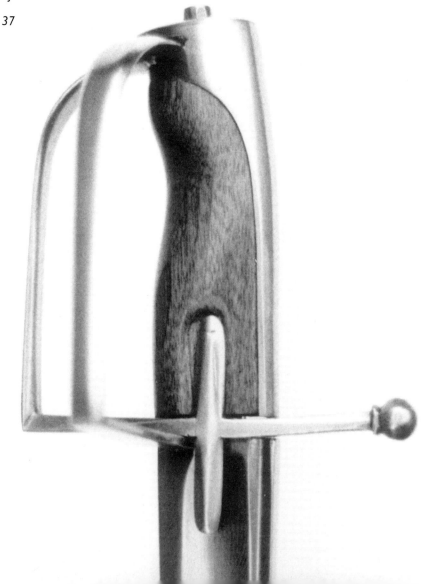

2-Bar form of 1788 pattern
Illustration 38

The sword hilt shown is a little known variant of the 1788 pattern in which the guard protection has been enhanced by the addition of a broad diagonal bar joining knucklebow to baseguard. The grip is of fishskin with copper wire binding. The blade is curved, broad fullered and has no decoration or manufacturer's marks.

Blade length   32.5in (82.5cm)
Sword weight   1lb 15oz (0.89kg)

2-Bar form of 1788 pattern

38

Light Cavalry sabres c. 1792-1796
Illustration 39

This type of sabre is probably unique in European sabre hilt form and appears to have been in limited use in the British Cavalry. The hilt form is distinctive and instantly recognizable. The recognition features are the extended fabricated pommel with an upper plate projecting over the 'D' knucklebow juncture, the large rounded-off, diamond shaped langets (which usually bear regimental markings) and pyramidal finial to the quillon. The grip is of hard wood with a cross-hatched surface. The example shown is etched with 'LDR' on one langet and the top plate of the pommel, probably denoting the Lanark and Dumfries Regiment (Scottish Yeomanry). The blade is undecorated, curved, single edged, bi-fullered with false edge and clipped point.

Blade length	36.5in (92.7cm)
Sword weight	1lb 12oz (0.8kg)

A number of other regiments are recorded using this type of sabre; 7th Light Dragoons, 10th Light Dragoons, 30th Light Dragoons, Leeds Light Dragoons and Warwick Light Dragoons.

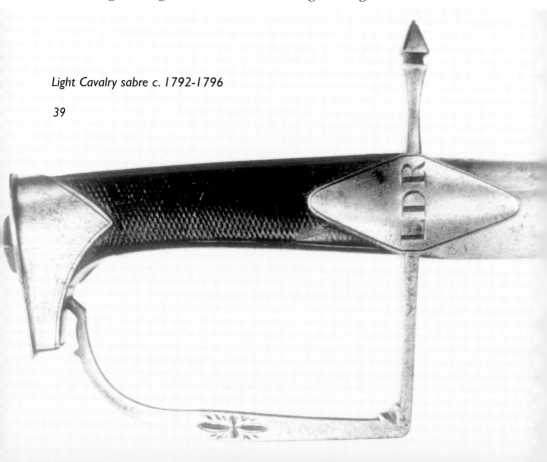

Light Cavalry sabre c. 1792-1796

39

Simple Light Cavalry sword c. 1792-1796
Illustration 40

7th Light Dragoons
c. 1792

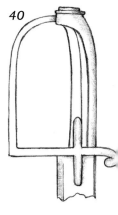

Whilst it is recorded in this period that the 7th Light Dragoons used the type of sword in illustration 39, the 1914 published Regimental History of the 7th Queen's Own Hussars records that their first light cavalry sword was one with the hilt form shown now in illustration 40. The guard is a simple 'D' knucklebow with double langets and quillons, a slim grip (disproportionate to the width of the blade) retained over the tang by a combined flattened pommel backstrap. The blade appears to be straight with either a flattened wedge section, or with a broad shallow fuller. The date of introduction into the regiment was not determined, but the sword is dated 1794, and was supplied by Wooley & Co, Birmingham. The blade is etched on one side with a crown over 7 L.D over Q.O and on the other side with a crown over G.R. There is also a mark of a crown over I.F. thought at that time to be a manufacturing mark, but more likely to be an inspection mark.

This sword was 'in possession of the Mess' at the time of publishing and was further corroborated by the possession of a coloured illustration of an officer of the regiment dated 1793 wearing this type of sword. There were criticisms of the sword in that the grip probably lacked strength and retention, and that the knucklebow (and subsequently for the 1796 pattern sabre) was 'practically useless', compared with the basket guard protection of the preceding dragoon swords (Illustrations 24 and 27).

1796 pattern Light Cavalry sword

The 1796 pattern Light Cavalry Sword, or sabre, is the sword that most people in Britain would recognize as a cavalry sabre and relate, with some certainty, to the Napoleonic wars, not only in Britain, but in Europe where the battles were fought. This is demonstrated in the Army Museum of Brussels which has one hall where hundreds of these swords, reputedly recovered from Waterloo, cover every foot of wall up to the lofty height of the ceiling. This weapon was produced in the thousands by British and German manufacturers and contractors, and, as a consequence a considerable number of variations are noticeable. Both officers, and other ranks' swords were of the same form in principle, the officers' swords having fishskin grips with wire binding and decorated blades, whilst other ranks had swords with leather grips and plain blades. It was not unusual however for the officers to have had preferences, and to make changes, such as leather covered grips. The Pattern was devised with some thought towards cutting ability, the blade being of a light falchion form where the weight could be concentrated into the last 8in towards the point to give some considerable impetus in the swing to make the cutting action more effective. Examples of the standard forms, and some variants can be shown.

Rounded Pommel-Backstrap
Illustration 41

Shows the standard form of hilt in its simplest form by which this Pattern is generally identified: a combined pommel and backstrap in rounded form with inner and outer ears about the grip through which passes a pin to secure the grip over the blade tang; a stirrup guard secured at the top of the tang and through the baseguard, and two langets projecting out over the blade, and an extended quillon. The example shown is an officer's sword with fishskin covered grip bound in silver wire, all hilt furnishings in steel. The curved blade is marked on the backstrap with 'J.J.Runkel, Solingen', and is decorated on both sides with gilt etchings:

    i) GR, Crown, Stand of Arms and foliage.

    ii) Royal Coat of Arms with 'Honi Soit qui Mal y Pense' and 'Dieu et mon Droit'.

Blade Length	32.75in (83.2cm)
Sword weight	1lb 13oz (0.83kg)

Rounded Pommel-Backstrap.

41

Facetted Pommel-Backstrap
Illustration 42

Is another officers' sword of later date and better quality. In this case the grip is leather covered with silver wire binding, and incorporates ground facets to the steel hilt furniture. The blade is gilt etched:

i) 'W&S Dawes – Birmingham' and 'Warranted', which limits the date of manufacture to between 1800 and 1812.

ii) A mounted dragoon with Tarleton helmet, GR, Crown, a Stand of Arms with Union shield, Union Jack, light cavalry sword hilt and Tarleton helmet and floral decoration.

iii) Britannia, Royal Coat of Arms, urn with floral spray.

Blade length   32.5in (82.5cm)
Sword weight   1lb 13oz (0.83kg)

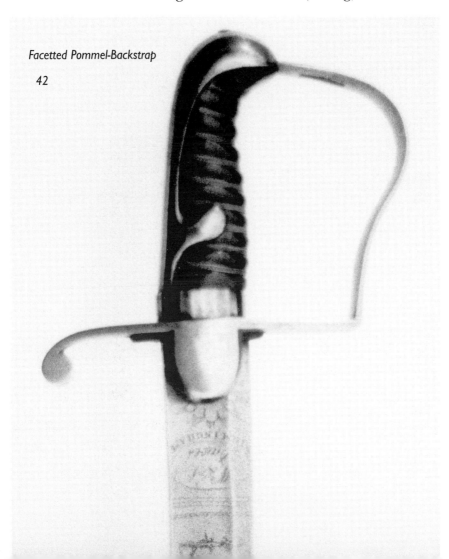

Facetted Pommel-Backstrap

42

Acanthus decorated hilt
Illustration 43

Shows the sword of a cavalry Colonel. The hilt furniture is in gilded copper decorated throughout with Acanthus foliage. The grip is covered with white sharkskin, bound in copper and silver wire. The blade, which has suffered from some degradation, has many etchings, some of which are not immediately interpretable, but illustrate the extent to which cavalry officers of this period were prepared to have their swords decorated:

i) An oval cartouche giving the manufacturers details; 'Osborne & Gunby – Sword Cutlers – to his Majesty – the Rt.Honble. Board of Ordnance – and the Hon. East India Compy – Birmingham & Pall Mall, London – Double Proof'. This would put the date of manufacture between 1808 and 1820.

ii) An indistinct form of Hope; 'Col. Barlow' in a ribboned cartouche over a Stand of Arms and armour, Britannia, the Barlow (London) family crest of a double headed griffin and the family motto (not readable) and a horn of plenty, and foliage.

iii) Foliage; 'For King and Country' in a ribbon cartouche, Royal Coat of Arms, Britannia and foliage.

Blade length	33in (83.8cm)
Sword weight	1lb 14oz (0.85kg)

Acanthus decorated hilt

43

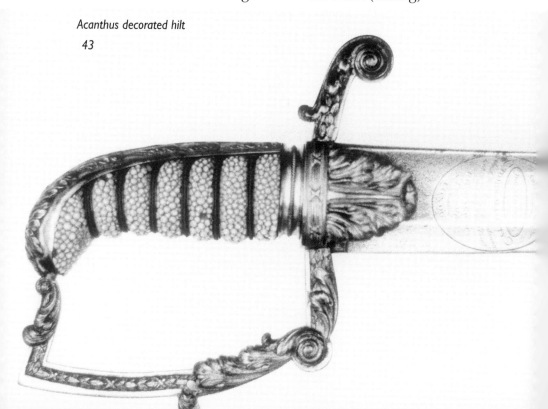

General Officer Commanding
Illustration 44

A sword for a General Officer Commanding. The hilt furnishings are in gilded copper, with acanthus decoration to the knucklebow, horizontal and diagonal striations to the pommel / backstrap, and lions' heads to the langets. The grip is covered in leather, bound in brass wire, and extended outwards below the pommel. The blade is plain, with the exception on one side of a cartouche containing two sets of foliage about a ribbon with 'OSBORN'S WARRANTED', setting the date of manufacture to between 1803 to 1807. Osborn is also stamped on the back edge.

Blade length	32.75in (83.2cm)
Sword weight	2lb 2oz (0.95kg)

General Officer Commanding

44

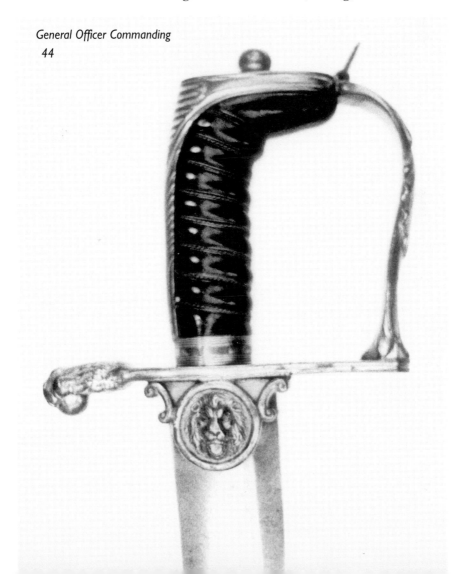

E.I.C. sabre
Illustration 45

A sword of heavy construction, possibly for an officer of the East India Company, plain leather covered grip. There are no manufacturers' marks, but the blade is extensively decorated without gilding or blueing:

i) Scrolling acanthus foliage, a Stand of Arms with central masked parade helmet; a lions head surmounted by scrolling foliage, palms and oak leaves.

ii) A crouching lion guarding a Union Shield in front of palms, foliage, and the initial 'G.W; a Stand of Arms about a parade armour breastplate and foliage.

Blade length	33.13in (84.2cm)
Sword weight	1lb 15oz (0.88kg)

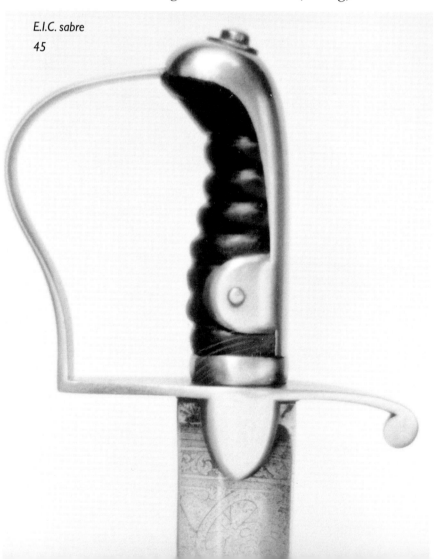

E.I.C. sabre

45

Yeomanry sabre
Illustration 46

An officers' sword possibly for a Yeomanry regiment, with copper gilt furniture and cross hatched ivory grip. The blade has a greater curve than normal, and 50 per cent of its length is composed of blued and gilt etchings:

i) A Stand of Arms, GR, Crown and foliage.

ii) A Stand of Arms with a cavalry helmet and Union Flag, Royal Coat of Arms and foliage.

Blade length	30.35in (76.8cm)
Sword weight	1lb 13oz (0.83kg)

Yeomanry sabre

46

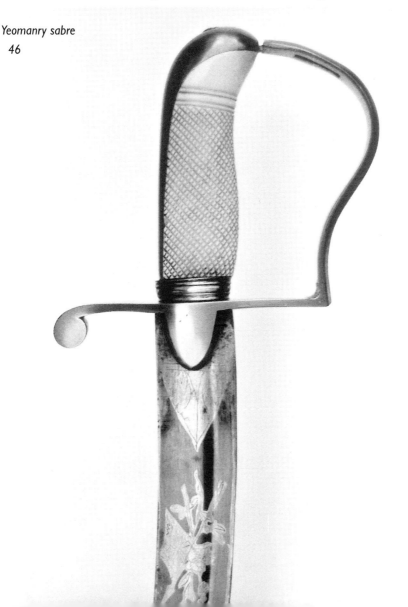

Yeomanry sabre
Illustration 47

An officers' sword for a Yeomanry regiment, with copper gilt furniture and leather covered copper wire bound grip. The blade is profusely etched, over 66 per cent of the blade length, without blueing or gilding:

i) Extensive acanthus scrolling foliage, a Stand of Arms with Union Flag about a studded targ and various foliage forms about a rose.

ii) Various forms of foliage, a Stand of Arms with Union Flag about a drum and acanthus foliage.

Blade length	29.75in 76.1cm)
Sword weight	1lb 5oz (0.6kg)

Yeomanry sabre

47

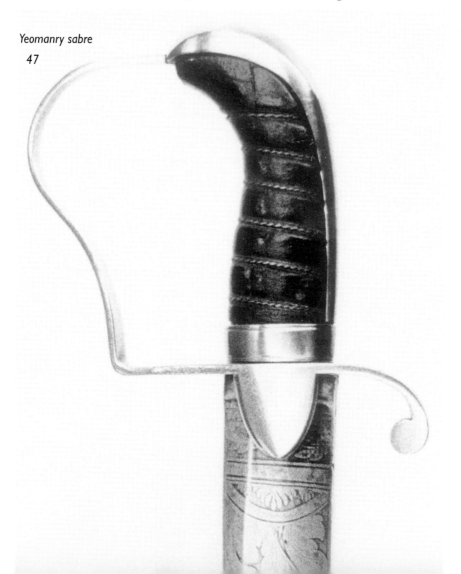

Horsehead Yeomanry sabre
Illustration 48

This is a Yeomanry Officers' sword dated '1799'. It was not uncommon for officers of Yeomanry Regiments to adopt the head of a horse as the pommel for the hilt. The example shown has hilt furnishings in bronze with a second variant of an added curved front side bar into the guard structure, and foliage decoration to the ferrule and quillon. The grip is leather covered and bound in copper wire. The blade is curved, broad fullered and spear pointed. There are no manufacturer's marks, but the blade is gilt decorated under a dark patina:

   i) '1799' The date within an oval and a mounted cavalryman.
   ii) Stand of Arms and GR.

Blade length	32.5in (82.5cm)
Sword weight	1lb 15oz (0.88kg)

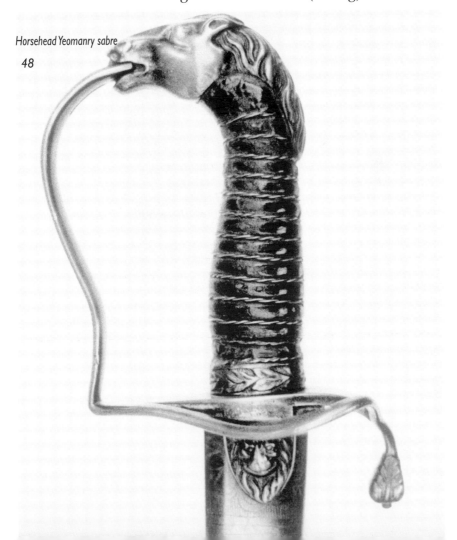

Horsehead Yeomanry sabre

48

Indian 1796 variant
Illustration 49

This is an unusual 1796 form that has been attributed to both Infantry and British raised Indian Cavalry regiments. The 'D' knucklebow has 'recessed' corners, both knucklebow and pommel/backstrap being chiselled with parallel grooving. The langets are of a scallop shell urn form; the grip is covered in fine grey fish skin, with three rosettes either side to secure the pins passing through the blade tang. The blade is highly polished, of a flattened triangular cross section, and with a 10in straight raised false edge.

The engravings on the blade can be summarised :

i) Manufacturers details: 'Cooper & Bank's – Warranted' in a ribbon cartouche, which probably dates the sword between 1815 and 1820.

ii) A Stand of Arms about a targ, with cavalry helmet and an entwined laurel wreath.

iii) Foliage, a laurel wreath and a Stand of Arms about two drums and foliage.

Blade length   31in (78.78cm)

Sword length   1lb 14oz (0.85kg)

Indian 1796 variant

49

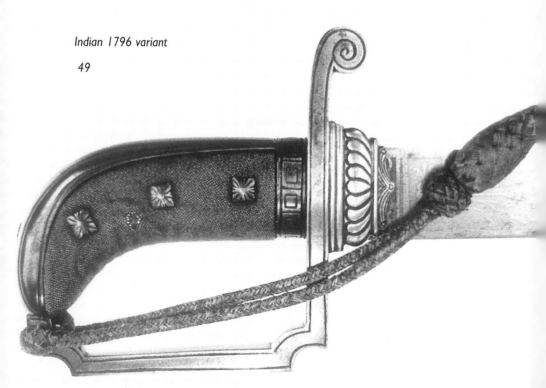

Transitory swords leading into 1821

Substantial changes were to take place in 1821, the formal date for the next Light Cavalry Sword Pattern. Leading into that date a number of exploratory changes were also taking place to the sword form which are worth noting.

3-Bar hilt variation
Illustration 50

This sword employs the principle of the curved sabre blade, but with a 2-Bar scrolled hilt. The grip is ribbed and leather covered, the pommel / backstrap facetted in form. A regimental motif of a crown with three Prince of Wales feathers within a circular ring is held between the two scrolled bars (this particular form of 2-Bar hilt may have originated as a regimental peculiarity with the 1788 pattern, the author being aware of two such examples in existence). The blade is etched in cavalry form:

i) Mounted cavalry man with Tarleton helmet, GR, a laurel wreath, crown and foliage.

ii) Britannia, Royal Coat of Arms and foliage.

Blade length	30.25in (76.8cm)
Sword weight	1lb 13oz (0.83kg)

3-Bar hilt variation

50

Movable Inner Knucklebow Illustration 51

This sword employs the basic 1796 hilt furniture, but with an added movable inner knucklebow, with a grip of ribbed horn. The blade however, has a piped back extending down to the point, curved, plain and has a re-curving raised false edge of 12^1/$_4$in. There are no manufacturers' marks.

Blade length	33.25in (84.5cm)
Sword weight	1lb 13oz (0.83kg)

Scrolled hilt Illustration 52

This sword uses the same form of knucklebow similar to the one on page 72, but to which is screwed an additional scrolled 2-Bar guard. The grip is of fish skin bound in copper wire, with combined stepped pommel and backstrap. The blade is pipe backed, plain (may have been etched, but degraded) and slightly curved with a spear point.

Blade length	35.38in (89.8cm)
Sword weight	1lb 12oz (0.84kg)

Movable inner 51
knucklebow

Scrolled hilt 52

Chapter 5

1780 – 1796 HEAVY CAVALRY

Whereas the preceding period of 1700 to 1780 had been a time of diversity and some uniqueness in cavalry hilt form, the approach to 1780 began to settle into some uniformity. For example, hilts with slotted baseguards found favour and presaged the 1788 Troopers' Pattern and basket guards took a more open form of curved bars. Towards the end of the century the hilt forms were to be considerably simplified for reasons of economy and ease of production.

Early slotted hilt c.1770
Illustration 53

Shows a heavy cavalry sword which originated about 1770 and continued through to about 1788, based on the simple Walloon branched knucklebow but the shell guards replaced with a slotted baseguard. This one piece structure was formed in thick iron and is relatively heavy compared with the earlier Walloon sword hilts. The pommel is heavy ovoid shape with a fish skin covered grip devoid of binding wire. The 33.25in (84.5cm) blade is wider than normal, straight and bi-fullered leading from a plain forté of 5in into a slightly tapering spear point. The sword weight is 2lb 8oz (1.15kg), and would have been for troopers. About the same time an officers' sword would have had a hilt of much more intricate design such as that shown in Illustration 54.

Early slotted hilt c.1770

53

Writhen Basket hilt c.1760

This illustration can only show an indicative part of the curved bar structure, which is presumed to have been damaged in action, but retained sufficient of the protective basket to allow its continued use. The hilt furniture is of gilded copper with a hemispherical whorled pommel securing a writhen basket of 3-bar structure, short interconnecting bars and an upper rein ring. The base guard is formed from shaped radiating bars. The spiralling formed grip is fish skin covered without wire binding. The blade is straight, bi-fullered, slightly tapering to a spear point, of length 31.5in (80cm); the sword weight is 2lb 2oz (0.95kg). The hilt forms of Illustrations 53 & 54 predict the definition of the form of the 1788 Heavy Cavalry pattern swords, and originate about 1760.

The 1788 Heavy Cavalry patterns
Illustration 54

The swords of both Troopers and Officers for the first recognized regulation pattern for the Heavy Cavalry were basically the same, although the officers' swords would have had more intricate designs around the hilt (as in Illustration 54) and some decoration to the blade.

Writhen basket hilt c.1760.

54

Basic form of 1788 pattern
Illustration 55

Basic form of 1788 pattern

55

Shows the plain form of the troopers' sword hilt, in which the base guard is slotted, the basket being of an open curved bar form, built up from a Walloon branched knucklebow, with two additional parallel curved bars either side of the grip, each bar linked with one small recurving bar. The pommel is of an extended urn shape, the grip is leather covered and wire bound. The blade is straight, broad fullered, and slightly tapering to a shallow spear point. The forté back edge bear a small impressed triangular mark.

> Blade length
> 33.88in (85.8cm)
> Sword weight
> 2lb12oz (1.25kg)

The 1796 Heavy Cavalry patterns

The abrupt change to new patterns after an interval of only eight years was probably necessitated by the Napoleonic Wars and the need to produce cheaper but serviceable weapons with an economy of purpose, particularly for the troopers of the many cavalry and yeomanry regiments being raised, or being brought up to war time levels for the campaigns in Europe, or to defend our shores from the threat of invasion. The patterns adopted were a complete departure from those accepted for 1788 and the diversity of designs experienced back to 1700.

Trooper Disc hilt pattern   Illustration 56
This illustration shows the recognized standard pattern hilt as manufactured in mass production by standard components, and popularly know as the Disc Hilt. This hilt truly portrays the economic benefits gained from mass production and simplicity, particularly towards inter-changeablity for removal and replacement of damaged parts. The disc, or base guard, is a simple circular plate complete with knucklebow and quillon stamped out as one piece, the stamping action also taking out fourteen holes in the plate, eight of which were for lightening, two to accommodate the langets when fitted, two for the blade tang, and two to take pins to secure a stiffening plate in position. A second operation radiused and bent the knucklebow portion of the plate to form the disc guard.

A second, or stiffening plate, diamond shaped with quillon, and three holes to take tang and pins, was stamped out and pinned to the disc guard. The remaining standard components, a ferrule and a combined pommel and backstrap with locating ears (from polished castings), and a preformed ribbed grip with leather covering, could then be slid over the tang, located at the pommel and pinned to the tang to secure the hilt in position. The combined pommel and backstrap was a distinguishable and common feature to the 1796 series of both heavy and light cavalry swords alike, although there were minor differences in fitting ability between the different manufacturers that could be catered for by the Regimental armourers. In the service life of this sword it was not unusual to remove the langets, or to cut away the inner section of the disc (to prevent wear to clothing). The blade was, in effect, straight, the last 7in being slightly angled backwards, broad fullered and hatchet pointed. Again, in service, the hatchet point may have been converted to a spear point. For the particular sword illustrated, the langets have been removed, but the hatchet point has been retained. The blade is stamped 'Dawes, Birmingham' on the back edge, and stamped with a crown over arrow within the fuller.

Blade length	34.8in (88cm)
Sword weight	2lb 5oz (1.05kg)

Disc hilt variation Illustration 57
The variation occurs to the form of the combined backstrap and the shape of the grip. The pommel is defined by a diagonal depression in the casting, which has allowed the manufacturer to

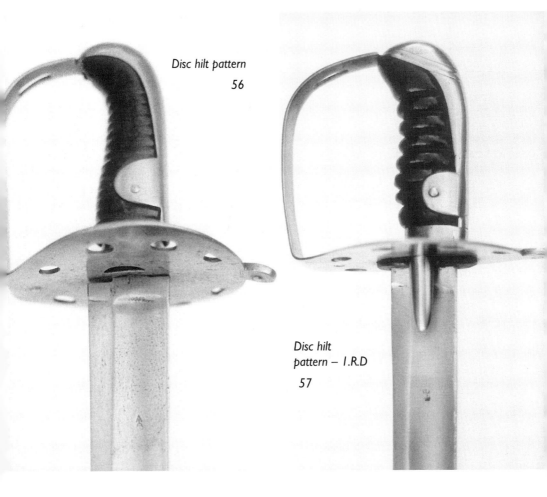

Disc hilt pattern

56

Disc hilt pattern – I.R.D

57

fit a more robust ribbed leather covered grip shaped to the contours of the hand within a space of 4 ¹/₄ in. These two variations appear to have been confined to the sword of the 1st Royal Dragoons, their identification being heavily etched upon the front face of the knucklebow – '1/E.55'. In this instance the inner edge of the disc has been cut away, but the langets have been retained. The blade is straight spear pointed, and marked with a crown/arrow. The Royals had their moments of glory at Waterloo, capturing the Eagle of the French 105th Regiment of the Line, and unremittingly charging the French Cuirassiers at Waterloo.

Blade length	34.3in (87cm)
Sword weight	2lb 2oz (0.96kg)

Officers' 1796 pattern, honeysuckle base
Illustrations 58i & 58ii

Portray a typical officers' sword built to the 1796 Heavy Cavalry Officers' pattern, in which both ferrule and combined pommel backstrap are formed with facetted surfaces. The grip is fish skin covered and wire bound. The guard is a one piece casting, the base bears a cut away honeysuckle design, a central urn like motif, leading into a broad knucklebow with a cut-out ladder effect. The blade is straight, broad fullered, spear pointed, each side covered in gilt etched decoration:

i) Foliage, crown and Royal Coat of Arms above a lion and foliage with a rose.

ii) Foliage, crown and GR and foliage.

Blade length	36.25in (91.4cm)
Sword weight	2lb 1oz (0.93kg)

58(i)

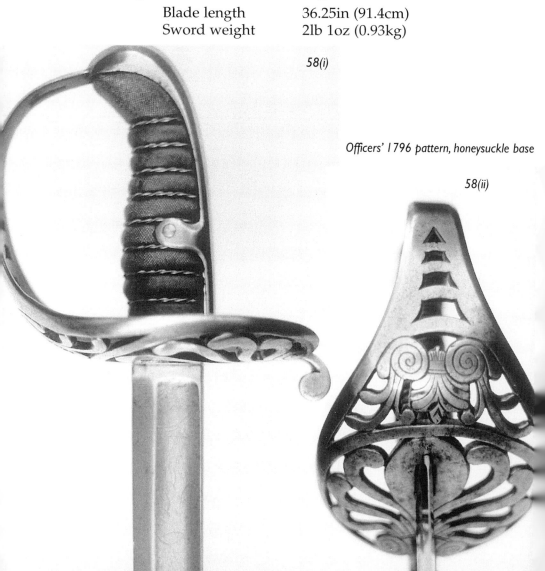

Officers' 1796 pattern, honeysuckle base

58(ii)

About this time two other swords were introduced for Troopers of the Heavy and Household Cavalry:

Life Guards, 1788-1812
Illustration 59
The Household Cavalry Museum (1971) displayed a sword of this type, listing it as 'a Rank and File Broadsword of the Lifeguards, 1788-1812', a sword that shows the characteristics of the 1796 Pattern, but with all the hilt furniture in brass (possibly for ceremonial use), the combined pommel backstrap closely following the 1796 eared form, the guard being a shallow bowl with sixteen triangular cut outs around the periphery, leading into a broad knucklebow with three 'ladder' cut outs. The grip is leather covered over cord ribs, the blade being hatchet pointed. For the sword illustrated the fuller has an impressed mark of a crown over arrow.

Blade length	35.25in (89.5cm)
Sword weight	2lb 12oz (1.25kg)

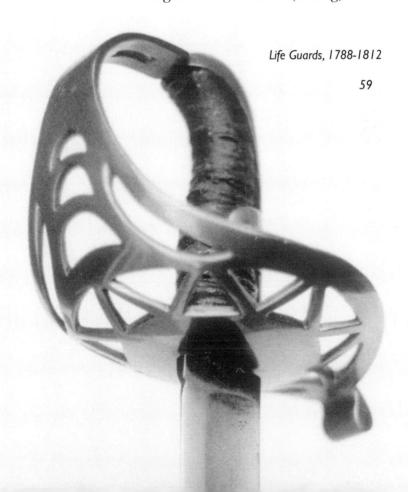

Life Guards, 1788-1812

59

Heavy Cavalry and RHG
Illustration 60

This sword is very similar to that shown in Illustration 58, except that the knucklebow branches are accentuated into large recurving bars in the Walloon style, and the hilt furniture is in steel. The supposition is that this form of sword may have been a Household Cavalry Service sword for Rank and File pre 1802. (The Household Cavalry Museum records that the regulation 1796 Heavy Cavalry Troopers sword was 'adopted' by the Royal Horse Guards in 1802, and taken into general use by the Household Cavalry from 1812 to 1832.) For the sword illustrated the identification markings on the blade back edge have been obscured by abrasive cleaning.

Blade length	34.63in (88cm)
Sword weight	2lb 2oz (0.95kg)

Heavy Cavalry and RHG

60

Chapter 6

THE TRANSIENT CELTIC HILT

There was no doubt that the Napoleonic Wars had demonstrated the worth of the 1796 Pattern swords, in particular the light cavalry sabre which was acclaimed for its cutting ability, and in spite of the limitations attributed to the disc-hilted heavy cavalry troopers' sword that caused the changes to take place to its guard and blade. The officers' heavy cavalry sword had also undergone some criticisms in that the broad fullered blade as produced, was considered to be too lightweight and flexible for a proper thrusting action, and not able to match the heavyweight brass hilted thrusters that were by now in universal use in the French Cavalry. Research by the Board of Ordnance was in progress, but slow to find solutions; a number of British manufacturers sought to influence the Boards with new designs of their own, hoping that they would be taken up as the new regulation patterns for the expected peace time Army. These swords were distinguishable from the existing cavalry swords, and from those that actually followed in 1821, having one feature in common, that of a shallow bowl hilt with line decoration of designs that can be traced back to the Celtic decoration of personal wear and religious significance, uncovered from the many excavations and researches into Celtic lore and mythology that were taking place at that time. The extent of manufacture of these swords was transient, experimental, and indeterminate, but worthy of consideration in any history or research into British Cavalry Swords. The three examples shown in this section are indicative of the priority given, at that time, to the development of a thrusting sword, principally for cavalry use.

Osborne and Gunby 'Celtic hilted' thrusting sword
Illustrations 61i, 61ii and 61iii

This rather spectacular sword was produced by Osborne and Gunby just after the turn of the nineteenth century, and was based upon the French heavy cavalry thrusting swords then in common use. The combined pommel and eared backstrap was common to all the 1796 patterns now in use by the British cavalry, securing a long (4.5in) grip with leather covering and brass wire binding. The bowl guard is large with single line peripheral decoration and a double line about the blade entry point, and central paralleled lines leading into a pair of Celtic whorls and one teardrop cutout. The intriguing feature of this sword is the undoubted return to a cross guard supported on a thick ferrule, with forward and rear pointing quillons, one passing through the teardrop cutout, the second resting on the rear edge of the bowl.

The cross guard ferrule raises the cross guard bar about one inch above the inner surface of the bowl giving adequate finger control to one side, and thumb control through a depression formed on the other side. The blade is equi-bi-fullered for improved strength, single edged, tapering straight down to a shallow hatchet but strong thrusting point. The manufacturer, Osborn & Gunby, is stamped on the forté back edge. There are no Board of Ordnance marks, as would have been prevalent at the time. This sword was obviously intended for heavy cavalry use.

Blade length	37.81in (96cm)
Sword weight	2lb 9oz (1.55kg)

Osborne and Gunby 'Celtic hilted' thrusting sword

61i

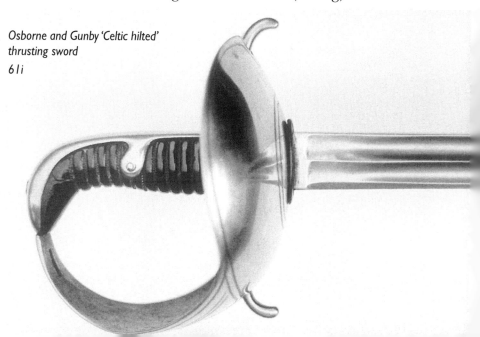

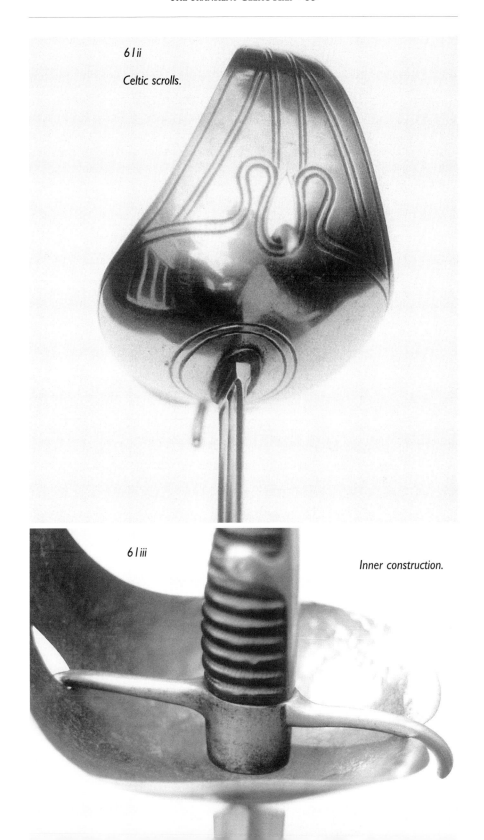

61 ii

Celtic scrolls.

61 iii

Inner construction.

Broadsword bladed Celtic hilt
Illustrations 62i and 62ii

This sword has no manufacturers' marks. The extended pommel/backstrap has no ears but still resembles the latter earlier pattern form. The grip is fish skin covered and silver wire bound. The shallow bowl has a single peripheral line, ending in whorls towards the rear quillon, and double lines surrounding the blade entry point, with five cut-out and line decoration that define a double whorl Celtic pattern. The blade is a double-edged, bi-fullered, broadsword in form with an armour piercing hatchet point. This form of sword would have been adequate for both thrusting and cutting action, and being much lighter was probably intended for light cavalry use.

Blade length
34.25in (87cm)
Sword weight
2lb 2oz (0.95kg)

62ii

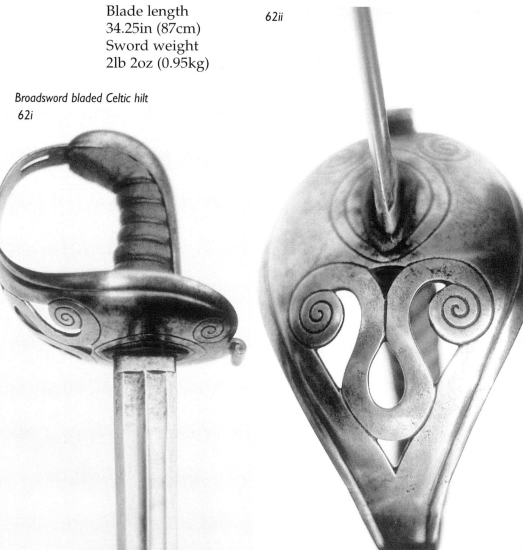

Broadsword bladed Celtic hilt
62i

Prosser Celtic hilted sword and blade
Illustrations 63i, 63ii and 63iii

This third sword is the 1819 patent by Prosser, based upon a heavy pipe-backed blade not in common use at the time, but which would have been considered suitable for both cut and thrust action. The combined pommel backstrap is again extended to define a pommel with flattened sides and stepped upper layers. The grip is fish skin covered with multi wire silver binding. The bowl is decorated in the same manner as in Illustration 62. The bowl is distinctive in that the last 13in is slightly recurving with a pronounced clipped back edge extension, a feature that Prosser was to carry through into the 1821 pattern swords of his manufacture. A peculiarity of this sword is the backward angle of the grip to the blade. Robson shows a sword of this type with battle honours of the 4th Light Dragoons, and was presumably made specifically for an officer.

| Blade length | 35in (88.9cm) | |
| Sword weight | 2lb 4oz (1.02kg) | 63iii |

Prosser Celtic hilted sword and blade

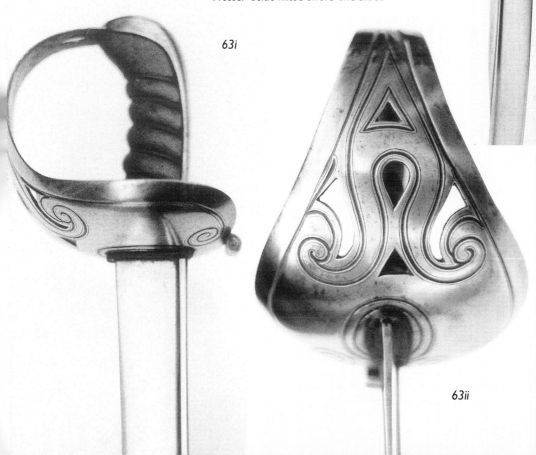

63i

63iii

63ii

Chapter 7

THE 1821 HEAVY CAVALRY PATTERNS

The deliberations and researches by the Boards of Ordnance to find the successors to the 1796 patterns resulted in a system that paired some sword components of the two Cavalry corps. For example, the blades for both Heavy and Light Cavalry Officers were now to follow the same basic form; that is pipe backed, same length, same slight curvature, and same weight. Similarly the blades for Other Ranks, although fullered, were also the same. Again this should have given some economy in manufacture and consistency of purpose, together with the theoretical benefits of interchangeability. For the officers the change to the 1821 patterns was one of relative elegance combined with an improved suitability for cut and thrust; for the rank and file the accent was again on relative simplicity, economy, and ability to cut and thrust.

Heavy Cavalry hilt forms can be typically shown as follows:

1821 Heavy Cavalry officers' pattern from 1821 to 1887
Illustrations 64i and 64ii

1821 Heavy Cavalry officers' pattern from 1821 to 1887.
64i

The shallow bowl guard is cut out overall in a continuous Honeysuckle motif which is the distinguishing feature of this type of sword hilt, a motif which from now will be a standard feature on cavalry officers' swords with origins from the early 1700s. The rest of the hilt is built up from standard components to assist interchangeability for damage and repair: a ribbed ferrule, combined backstrap pommel with a defined stepped pommel section and a plain thumb rest towards the ferrule, and a wooden grip covered in fish skin bound in copper wire. The blade is pipe backed, devoid of any decoration, and only slightly curved to present a blade suitable for both cut and thrust. In this form the sword became the regulation undress pattern for Heavy Cavalry officers, and was favoured by the Household Cavalry as an officers' service sword.

Blade length	35.38in (89.75cm)
Sword weight	1lb 13oz (0.83kg)

1821 Heavy Cavalry officers' pattern from 1821 to 1887.

64ii

1821 Heavy Cavalry regimental sword of the 4th Royal Irish Dragoons. Illustrations 65i and 65ii

This sword was supplied by Chambers of Little Maddox Street, Bond Street, London who operated from that base between 1830 and 1852. The guard is larger that the standard form, and the pipe backed blade, complete with minor sword cuts, is embellished with decoration:

i) Crown/VR/Laurel wreath and a cartouche containing an oak branch with leaves and acorns.

ii) A cartouche containing '4th Royal Irish Dragoons' in a surround of laurel leaves and wreath and supplier's details.

This sword reflects the honour of bearing oaken remembrances that originated with the 1661 Lifeguard sword of Charles II; there is the possibility that it may have served in the Charge of the Heavy Brigade, 24 October 1854, where the 4th Dragoons (Guards) destroyed the Russian opposing flank.

Blade length	35.38in (89.75cm)
Sword weight	2lb 4oz (1.03kg)

Left: Regimental insignia.

65i

Right: Oakleaves and acorns.

65ii

1821 Heavy Cavalry regimental officers' sword c.1856
Illustration 66

This is the sword of Lieutenant Augustus W. Travers of the 5th Dragoon Guards, showing one or two differences to the standard hilt form; thumb rest and pommel head are chequered; the guard has a shallower bowl; a Wilkinson Patent Solid Hilt has been incorporated, i.e. the blade tang at the same width as the blade forté has been used as the basis of the grip which has then been pinned with shaped wood or leather strips and bound with wire to make a grip. Produced by Henry Wilkinson, No. 6880, the blade is only slightly curved, single fullered and tapering to a shallow spear point, and obviously intended as a 'thruster'. The blade surfaces have minimal decoration and information.

i) A ribbon cartouche with 'A.W. Travers – 5th Dragoon Guds.'; crown/VR/foliage.

ii) 'Henry Wilkinson, Pall Mall, London'; 'Patent Solid Hilt'; crown/VR/foliage.

This sword may have seen extended service by a descendant or other relative of A.W. Travers, having been coated with preservative paint, and further painted with khaki of the type used in the Boer War.

Blade length	36.13in (91.75cm)
Sword weight	2lb 0.5oz (0.92kg)

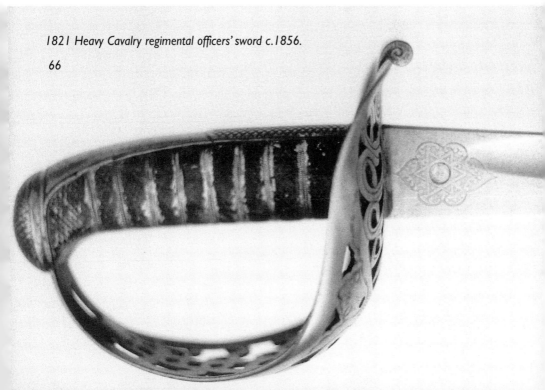

1821 Heavy Cavalry regimental officers' sword c.1856.

66

Heavy Cavalry Troopers' sword
Illustrations 67i and 67ii

Shows the standard form of hilt, in which the combined backstrap pommel follows the basic 1796 form, the lower section held by the ferrule, the larger ears pinned through the grip and the blade tang, but includes two minor changes in which a formed depression differentiates the pommel head from the rest of the component to conform with the officers' pattern. The grip is formed from wood and covered in black leather, somewhat worn. The solid bowl guard is shallow with a single line peripheral decoration leading into simple whorls at the quillon. This area of the bowl contains the stamped regimental information 'G. 5DG. 56', (i.e. 5th Dragoon Guards), and a vague 'S.S.' at the quillon. The blade is plain, without markings, slightly curved, single fullered, some sword cuts being apparent, the presumption being its use in the Charge of the Heavy Brigade, 24 October, 1854.

Blade length	36.13in (91.75cm)
Sword weight	2lb 6.5oz (1.09kg)

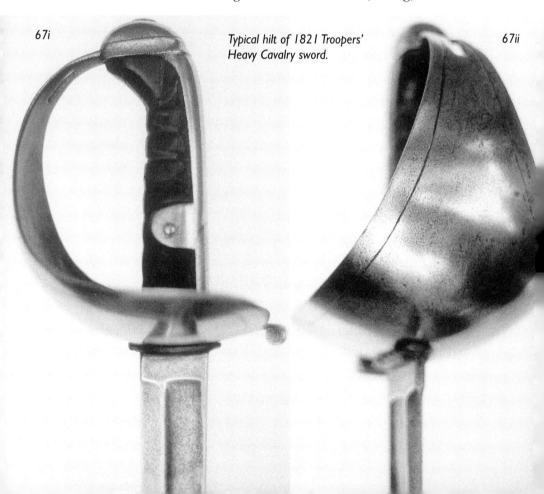

67i

Typical hilt of 1821 Troopers' Heavy Cavalry sword.

67ii

Composite/transient sword of the 6th Dragoons in the Crimea
Illustration 68

The change from the 1821 Troopers' sword to the Universal Trooper sword of 1853 was coincident with the Crimean War. Some cavalry regiments were sent to the Crimea with the 1821 patterns, a few with the new 1853 Pattern. One Regiment, the 6th Dragoons, however, appears to have been sent a conversion kit, some of the components being lost in transit, which was not unusual for the infamous logistics of the Crimean War. The armourers of the 6th

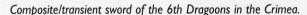

Composite/transient sword of the 6th Dragoons in the Crimea. **68**

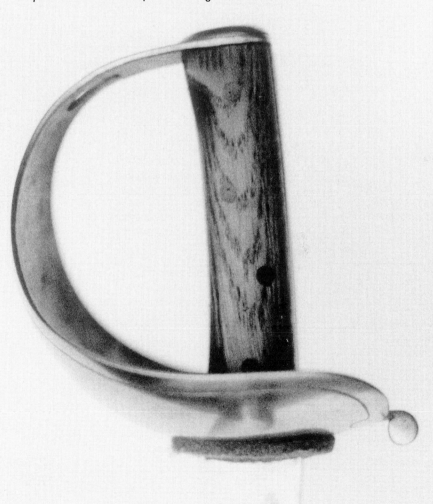

Dragoons therefore were given the task of assembling swords from what was available. The result was a sword built up from an 1853 blade with blade width tang fitted with leather grips pinned to the tang, but without the retention washers that prevented movement of the leathers, and the shallow bowl guard of the 1821 pattern (not the 3-Bar guard of the 1853).

The illustration shows such a sword hilt, but which has since been refurbished with oak grips following its service in the Crimea. In its case the 1821 bowl guard carries the markings of the 6th Dragoon Guards '87/6-D' above and below the sword knot aperture, and a small mark, possibly 'S.S.' at the quillon. The blade is slightly curved and fullered, with 'Enfield' stamped on the back edge, 'S.S.' on one side of the forté, and 'Crown/E/6' on the other.

Blade length	36.38in (92.4cm)
Sword weight	2lb 8oz (1.15kg)

A similar sword of the 6th Dragoons, but with the 1853 grip leathers more intact, and complete with white leather liner, was put up for sale by Wallis & Wallis in 1981. The scabbard bore an old engraving 'Balaclava, Octbr. 25th 1854'. The Regimental marking on the bowl was '243/6-D'. Both scabbard and blade forté were damaged, thought to have been caused by a shot. The 25 October 1854 was, of course, the day of the Charge of the Light Brigade. The work of the Heavy Brigade on that day was to take or harass the Russian redoubts south of the line taken by the Light Brigade Charge.

Chapter 8

THE 1821 LIGHT CAVALRY PATTERNS AND THEIR VARIATIONS

As with the Heavy Cavalry patterns, the 1821 Light Cavalry pattern swords were modeled with the paired blades of the heavies, but with dissimilar hilts, thus ensuring some differentiation between the two divisions in the cavalry. Whilst Heavy Cavalry officers of this time did not appear to develop or demand differences from their standard designs, there did appear to be that need amongst Light Cavalry officers to cater for their own preferences, some clearly preferring a thrusting sword to the stated cut and thrust, and for which the new regulation patterns had not been designed.

OFFICERS

1821 Light Cavalry officers' pattern from 1821 to c. 1850
Illustrations 69i, 69ii and 69iii

This original pattern was equipped with a slightly curved pipe backed blade, in every respect the same as that used for the 1821 Heavy Cavalry Officers' pattern, suitable for both cutting, and by virtue of the rigid pipe back, the thrusting action. However, whilst the heavy cavalry sword had a honeysuckle guard, the light cavalry form was built up from a bar knucklebow from which branch two parallel curved bars on the outside, and a small side bar on the other, to form a guard which is now generally known as a 3-Bar hilt. The combined backstrap pommel conforms to the general form of that for the heavy cavalry sword. The similarity between blades and backstrap pommels and grips now begins to demonstrate the gradual move towards an overall standardization of sword form and structure for the two divisions of cavalry, and to what might be termed the universal sword. For this sword as illustrated the blade is decorated only with a Crown over GR IV within a laurel wreath, the sole decoration allowed by the dress regulations at that time.

Blade length	36.0in (91.8cm)
Sword weight	1lb 10oz (0.85kg)

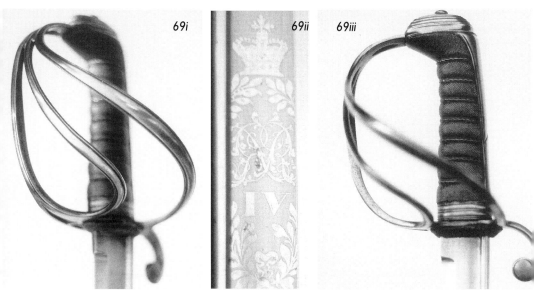

1821 Light Cavalry officers' variation, 1830 – 1837
Illustrations 70i, 70ii and 70iii

This sword was by Prosser, etched with the supplier details at the blade forté where there is a significant sword cut, which demonstrates the force by which the cutting action can be delivered, particularly at the charge. Again the sole decoration is a crown/WR IV/laurel wreath. The distinguishing feature of this sword is the raised back edge and recurving point identical to that used by Prosser in his 1819 Patent Celtic hilt sword. The hilt is also a variant from the standard form, having a grip of 5in which is longer than usual, and heavier bars to the guard, the whole appearance and feel of the sword being that it was intended to be for a heavy cavalryman on special order.

Blade length	35.38in (89.75cm)
Sword weight	2lb 4oz (1.03kg)

Light Cavalry officers' pattern from 1821 to c. 1850.

1821 Light Cavalry officers' regimental sword, 1850 – 1887
Illustrations 71i and 71ii

As with the Heavy Cavalry Officers version, the 1821 Light Cavalry Officers' pattern changed its structure by replacing the pipe backed blade with a single fullered blade possibly about 1850, the process of standardization having gone one stage further. The sword shown is that for the 11th Hussars, the only other identification that of a Proof Mark of the 6 pointed star of B. Thurkle, High Holborn, London. The backstrap pommel has a chequered thumb rest, the top of the pommel being stepped. The grip is fish skin covered, bound with silver wire. The blade is slightly curved with decoration at the forté and over the central half of the blade:

i) Foliage; crown/XI Hussars/laurel wreath, with foliage above and below.

ii) Two medieval soldiers with scrolling branches, foliage, crown/VR, with foliage above and below.

Blade length	34.56in (80.8cm)
Sword weight	1lb 13oz (0.83kg)

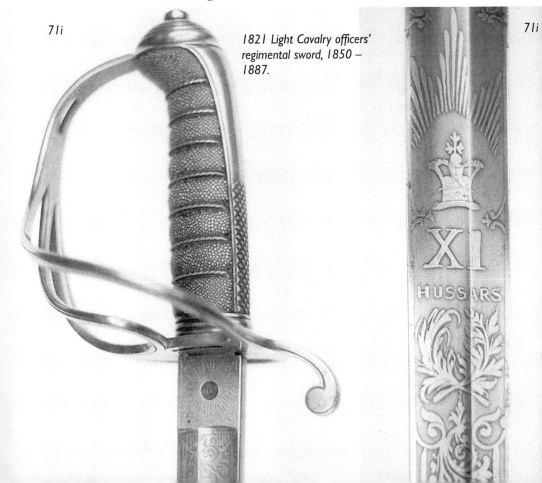

71i

1821 Light Cavalry officers' regimental sword, 1850 – 1887.

71i

1821 Light Cavalry officers' regimental sword c. 1886
Illustrations 72i, and 72ii

This sword incorporates the Wilkinson Patent Solid Hilt, in which the wider grip appears to be of a chequered composite nature, and bound with silver wire. The blade is slightly curved, plated, and stamped with the Wilkinson number 27268 on the back edge, and with embossed decoration overall:

i) Wilkinson details including 'By Appointment, Prince of Wales'; 17th Lancers motif of crossed lances with skull and crossed bones, 'Or Glory', '17th Duke of Cambridge Own Lancers'; crown/VR/with foliage above and below.

ii) Jessel Crest of a collared eagle/torch/Initials HMJ; crown/VR/with foliage above and below.

Blade length	35.1in (89.8cm)
Sword weight	2lb 3oz (0.98kg)

This sword was supplied to Herbert Merton Jessel when he joined the 17th Lancers in 1886, retiring as Captain in 1896, sometime Captain in the Royal Berkshire Yeomanry, sometime Hon. Colonel 1st Battalion City of London Royal Fusiliers, in between times Alderman and Mayor of Westminster 1902–3. He rejoined the Army in 1914 at the outbreak of war as a remount conducting officer, and appointed Lieutenant Colonel Commandant Remount Service in 1915, serving in France and Belgium, twice mentioned in dispatches, and reappointed Deputy Director of Remounts at the War Office with the rank of Colonel in 1918–19. Following his service he was honoured with the CMG in 1918, the CB (Mil) in 1919 and created Baron Jessel of Westminster in 1924.

Wilkinson patent hilt.

72i

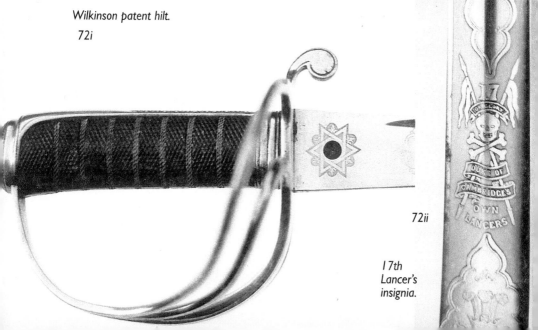

72ii

17th Lancer's insignia.

Victorian variation in the general form to the 1821 pattern
Illustrations 73i, and 73ii

This sword has no maker's identification marks other than the laurel wreath proof mark of silver, who operated from London and Liverpool. It is possibly unique in both its structure and its dedication, and obviously made to order for an individualistic cavalry officer. The hilt is atypical of the pattern, with the two curved bars being distributed equally about the grip, which is about 5in in length, covered in fish skin and bound with silver wire. The second variation is in the blade form, slightly curved, tapering to a shallow spear point, with a wedge shaped cross section that gives strength to the blade for the thrusting action. The blade is worn, but decorated overall, including a dedication to both the sword and its owner in the form of a patriotic poem:

> *A good man to wear me for Liberty and Right*
> *A strong hand to bear me for England to Fight*
> *A stout heart to back me in every good cause*
> *To fight for my Country, Her Honour and Laws.*

The other decorations consist of foliage, and urn with palms, a crown/VR.

Blade length   35.25in (89.5cm)
Sword weight 2lb 2oz (0.93kg)

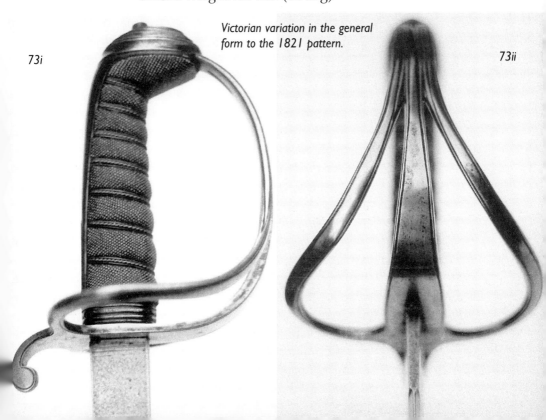

73i

Victorian variation in the general form to the 1821 pattern.

73ii

Yeomanry officer variation, 1848 Illustration 74

This is the sword of William Devereux Nicholls, Earl of Chester's Yeomanry Cavalry. It varies from the standard officers' sword of the period. The hilt modelled on the Troopers' sword with a longer, ribbed and leather covered grip and the blade is straight with bi-fullers which only start 4.5in from the grip, tapering over its length, and a false edge of 11in, to a shallow spear point, obviously made for thrusting in preference to cutting.

Blade length	34.5in (87.6cm)
Sword weight	1lb 13oz (0.98kg)

The blade bears a cartouche in the main fuller: 'William Devereux Nicholls – E.C.Y.C' who is recorded as entering the Regiment as a Cornet in 1848, and as Lieutenant with seniority from 15 April 1851, second senior officer of the Altrincham Troop.

Thrusting Sword Variation Illustration 75

This typical 3-Bar hilt officers' sword is fitted with an atypical blade of triangular cross section and tapering to an armoured piercing point. The blade, which is by 'Couleaux et Cie a Klingenthal' has no ability to cut and is a thruster, pure and simple.

Blade length	36.5in (92.7cm)
Sword weight	1lb10oz (0.73kg)

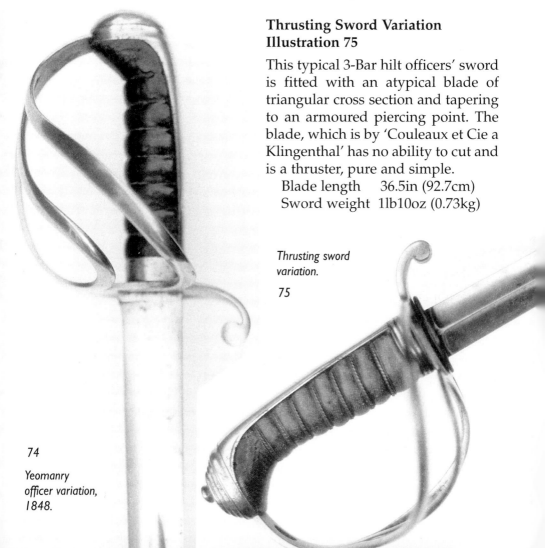

Thrusting sword variation.

75

74

Yeomanry officer variation, 1848.

Officers' second sword option
Illustration 76

It was not unusual for officers to buy second swords which could be used in an emergency if their usual fighting or service sword became too damaged or broken whilst campaigning abroad. Such swords may also have been termed 'civilian' swords, as they bore no military identification apart from a similarity to a current pattern. The sword shown is representative of the 1821 Light Cavalry pattern, but with black leather covered grip with brass wire binding, and a slightly curved single fullered blade. Lord Byron is reputed to have carried a similar sword in his wanderings in Greece and the Balkans. The blade bears the supplier details at the forté. 'Gilpin & Co., Northumberland St, Strand, London.' This supplier is not recorded as a regular supplier of military equipment.

Blade length   34.75in (88.25cm)
Sword weight 1lb 11oz (0.78kg)

RANK AND FILE

Pipe Backed 3-Bar hilt for NCOs
Illustration 77

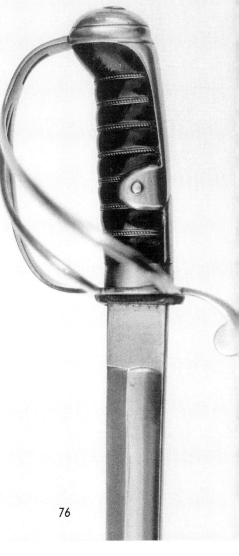

76

Officers second sword option.

There appear to be few examples of rank and file pipe backed cavalry swords. The illustration shows such a sword to the general form of the 1821 Light Cavalry Officers' pattern, but with ribbed black leather covered grip without wire binding, and the backstrap pommel with smooth finish but without the ears of the 1796 component of the Troopers' sword.

The side guard is hinged and spring loaded, capable of being lowered and locked to avoid scuffing to the clothing. The blade is shorter than the accepted pipe backed length, plain, and stamped with a drawn bow with arrow and the initials B.M. at one forté side, and a Board of Ordnance arrow over 'I' on the other.

Pipe Backed 3-Bar hilt for NCOs.

77

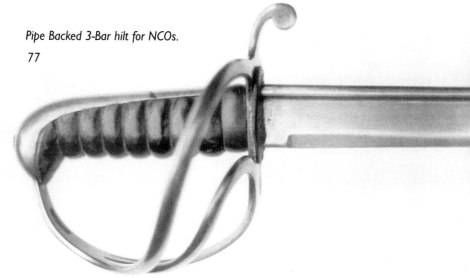

Blade length   33.25in (84.5cm)
Sword weight   1lb15oz (0.88kg)

The sword was manufactured by BLECKMANN of Solingen who undertook contracts from the British Government during the period 1858 to 1875 through their agents A.G. Franklin & Co. of London. Bleckmann was recognized as a specialist in small batch production quantities.

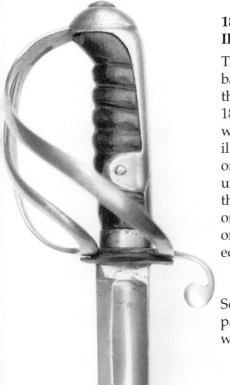

1821 Light Cavalry Troopers' sword
Illustration 78

This pattern closely follows the eared backstrap pommel, and fullered blade of the Heavy Cavalry Troopers' pattern for 1821, except that the bowl guard is replaced with a 3-Bar guard. For the sword illustrated, thought to have been 'passed on' to the East Kent Mounted Rifles, but unmarked as such except on the scabbard, the blade is stamped with an 'I' and a crown on one side of the forté, and a crown/BR (?) on the other. Residual markings on the back edge are obscured by cleaning.

Blade length   34.75in (88.3cm)
Sword weight   2lb 3oz (1.00kg)

Some German contract swords to this pattern are often found to be supplied with wire binding at the grip.

1821 Light Cavalry Troopers' sword of the Earl of Chester's Yeomanry Cavalry 1848 – 1851   Illustration 79

The sword hilt shown for this Regiment follows the general outline for all 1821 Light Cavalry Troopers' swords except for the manner in which the tang is secured at the pommel i.e. by forming the tang end over a larger, thicker washer, instead of over the pommel top itself. In this case the Regiment, Troop and the number of sword are stamped upon the base of the knucklebow: 'E.C.Y.C/D.9', which is not always apparent on light cavalry troopers' swords of the time. There are no manufacturers' markings on the blade.

79

1821 Light Cavalry Troopers' sword of the Earl of Chester's Yeomanry Cavalry 1848 – 1851.

Blade length   35.13in (89.2cm)
Sword weight   2lb 4oz (1.03kg)

The Earl of Chester's Yeomanry Cavalry had its beginnings as early as 1666 when Cheshire was required to form two troops of Light Horse, and became the premier yeomanry force in England from that time. They were, however, sorely treated in the matter of their exchange swords when regulations changed the patterns. Sadly when the 1796 pattern sabre changed to the 1821 pattern there was considerable delay with the E.C.Y.C, the Regimental History recording that in 1848, whilst the flint lock carbines had been exchanged fairly quickly to the 1844 percussion cap carbine (one of which is in the possession of the author), a considerable correspondence since 1839 had been entered into between the Regiment and the Board of Ordnance for the exchange of their 'unserviceable scimitars' for the new 1821 pattern sword. Eventually the Board of Ordnance agreed to an exchange, a batch being delivered sufficient for one troop in 1848, the balance being delivered in stages through to 1851, just two years before the expected change again to the 1853 pattern! At that time the Regiment consisted of eight Troops. The supplier of these swords was Lilly of Birmingham at a cost of twelve shillings and sixpence per sword. However, by the time of the Boer War, the process of pattern exchange had speeded up somewhat, a photograph c.1900 of a Cheshire (E.C.Y.C) Yeomanry Trooper in Parade Order outside Chester Cathedral clearly showing that he carried an 1899 pattern sword. With the commencement of the Boer War, the Cheshire Yeomanry supplied two companies, 21st and 22nd, for the Imperial Yeomanry.

PRIZE SWORD 2ND TROOP
WARWICKSHIRE YEOMANRY CAV
GIVEN BY BOLTON KING MAJOR
1845.

80i

Prize swords of this period

Prize swords were generally on offer within the regular cavalry and yeomanry regiments as an annual incentive in training in all aspects of the cavalry function for sword and shot and general aptitude. Some regiments adopted special patterns for these occasions, but usually a plain officers' sword of the period was used as the base, with added inscription and decoration to record the honour. Illustrations 80 (i) to (iii) inclusive show the inscription, recipient and type of decoration that was entered into for a prize sword of the Warwickshire Yeomanry Cavalry of 1845, with an 1821 Light Cavalry Officers' sword as a base:

i) Prize Sword awarded to 'Samuel Walker', in a Ribbon Cartouche.

ii) Inscription and Presentation 'Prize Sword 2nd Troop, Warwickshire Yeomanry Cvy, given by Bolton King, Major, 1845', in a Laurel Leaf surround.

iii) Mounted Cavalryman.

iv) A Stand of Country Farm implements surmounted by foliage and an urn with roses and thistles predominant, which denote a Yeomanry Regiment.

v) Profuse foliage with Sunflowers predominant.

vi) Crown/VR with laurel wreath and sunburst surround.

vii) A Stand of Arms, including a cavalry helmet and sword.

viii) At the forté, suppliers detail (Robert Mole of Birmingham) below a Stand of Ceremonial Flags, musicalia and honours, all surrounding a Cavalryman's helmet.

>   Blade length   35.63in (90.05cm)
>   Sword weight 1lb 12oz (0.8kg)

The 1858 Army List records Bolton King as being Lieutenant Colonel of the Regiment with seniority from 25 January 1848.

80ii

Inscription, recipient and type of decoration entered into for a prize sword.

80iii

Chapter 9

RANK AND FILE UNIVERSAL PATTERNS OF 1853 AND 1864

1853 saw the introduction of the first universal sword for both heavy and light divisions of the British Cavalry and all the other mounted Corps, with the exception of the Household Cavalry, who were to have a special sword. The concept of the universal sword was a compromise between the light cavalry 3-Bar hilt with modified solid grip based on the wider tang and leather outers, and a heavy cavalry blade that was capable of cutting, but whose prime intention was one of thrusting. The War Office records show that the preferred dimensions for this pattern were:
Blade length 35.5in (90.2cm)
Sword weight 2lb 7 3/4oz (1.13kg)

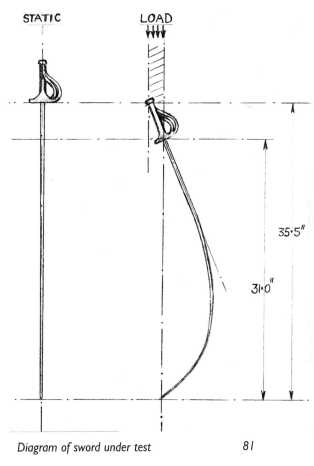

STATIC   LOAD

35·5"

31·0"

Diagram of sword under test   81

The testing of these swords was quite severe, to quote: 'The blade is subjected to a direct vertical pressure and until the distance from point to hilt, measured in a line, is reduced 4.5 inches'. Illustration 81, roughly to scale, shows what the bend in the blade may have looked like.

A number of swords to this pattern are shown to illustrate features of the standard pattern, their dimensions comparative to the optimum stated, plus two little known variations to the pattern.

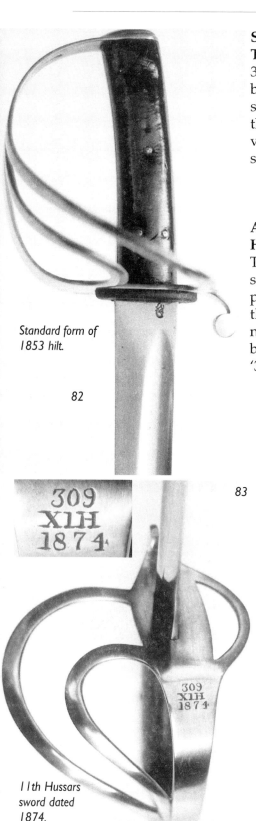

Standard form of 1853 hilt.

82

11th Hussars sword dated 1874.

Standard Form of 1853 pattern Troopers' sword Illustration 82

3-Bar hilt with plain polished bars, black leather chequered grips and a slightly curved fullered blade bearing the German Kirschbaum mark of a visored helmet at the forté on one side and a crown/32 on the other.

Blade length   35.5in (90.2cm)
Sword weight 2lb 7oz (1.11kg)

A Regimental sword of the 11th Hussars Illustration 83

This sword is of particular significance in that it records a particular moment in the history of the 11th Hussars, shown by the numbering and date etched at the base of the knucklebow '309/X1H/1874'.

Blade length   35.31in (89.3cm)
Sword weight 2lb 7oz (1.11kg)

There are no other identifications on the blade other than an 'Arrow/I' on the back edge.

On the conclusion of the Crimean War the 11th Hussars returned to England to reform and train, and undertake some service in Ireland, and were then sent to India in 1865, to remain there until 1877.

They were too late to rearm with the new 1864 pattern sword, but were not unduly worried, as rumour had it that the new sword would have been detrimental to their dress, which since the time of Cardigan had been a matter of pride and was to be maintained wherever they were stationed. The date 1874 commemorates their

83

review by the Prince of Wales (later King Edward VII) when he commended the Regiment's exemplary approach to its turnout and it meritorious activity in India.

A Yeomanry sword variation
Illustration 84

This sword has a blade decorated in the same manner for the 1821 Pattern Officers' swords:

i) Foliage surrounding a ribbon cartouche containing the yeomanry regimental identification 'WK.Q.O.Y Cavalry'.

ii) Foliage surrounding 'Crown/VR'

Otherwise, this sword of the Warwickshire Queen's Own Yeomanry Cavalry has no proof mark or manufacturer's marking and is in the standard form of the 1853 Troopers' pattern. The dimensions however are different:

Blade length	34.13in (86.7cm)
Sword weight	2lb 3oz (1.00kg)

Warwick Castle Variations

A visit to Warwick Castle in 1973 disclosed two swords hanging on a corridor wall similar to the 1853 pattern, both with 1853 3-Bar guards, both with solid grips but in a ribbed form as opposed to the standard flat chequered leather. The blades also differed, one being standard fullered blade, the second of a straight wedge cross-section form. The origin of these swords is not clear.

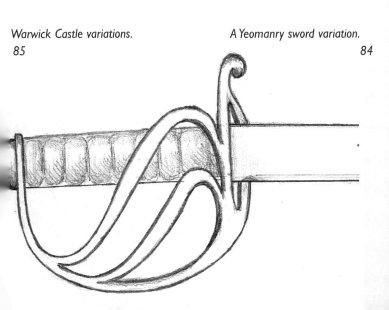

Warwick Castle variations.
85

A Yeomanry sword variation.
84

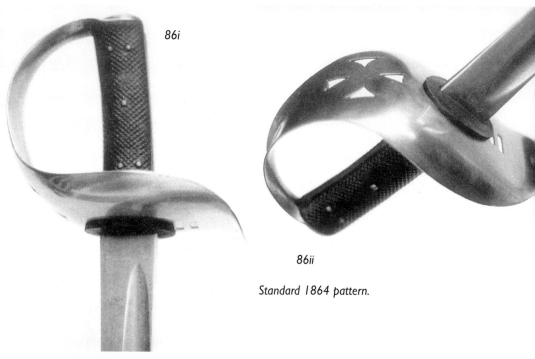

86i

86ii

Standard 1864 pattern.

Rank and File universal pattern of 1864
Illustrations 86i and 86ii

To overcome criticisms of handling for the 1853 pattern, which were not considerable, the War Office created a new pattern in 1864 which retained the 1853 blade exactly as it stood, the same principle of the solid grip with chequered leathers, but changed the 3-Bar guard for a bowl, larger than that used for the 1821 Heavy Cavalry Troopers' sword, but which blatantly ignored the problems attributed to the 1821 bowl and its reasons for changing to the 3-Bar hilt. The distinguishing features of this new bowl were the rolled rear edge, the double sword knot aperture in the bowl towards that rear edge and the representation of a Maltese Cross cut out of the bowl front. Some of these latter features were to be repeated in subsequent Troopers' patterns.

For the sword illustrated, the inside of the round edge is stamped with a 'Crown/B/21'. The blade back edge is marked 'Mole' and 'Crown/B/21', and the reverse forté is marked 'Robert Mole & Sons, Birmingham'.

Blade length   35.13in (86.7cm)
Sword weight   3lb 5oz (1.05kg)

Chapter 10

THE DRESS REGULATIONS OF 1857
(SCROLL HILT)

The precise reasoning behind the introduction of the new Scroll hilt for cavalry officers' swords as defined in the 1857 dress regulations to run in parallel with the 1821 honeysuckle and 3-Bar hilts, which were well established and accepted at that time, has never been made clear. The term 'Scroll' originates from the scrolled effect of the Acanthus foliage (thistle related) which has been used in classical ornamentation, most notably Grecian, for many hundreds of years, and is noticeably a more flamboyant style than that of the honeysuckle. The Scroll hilt as defined in 1857 clearly differentiates it from the existing honeysuckle form of the 1821 pattern for Heavy Cavalry officers. Charles Ffoulkes appears to be the first military arms author to have publicized the existence of the scroll pattern, including it in his *Arms and Armament* of 1945-47, showing one scroll hilt configuration in Figure 31.E for a Heavy Cavalry Officer of 1896. This may have inferred that the Scroll hilt was confined to the Heavy Cavalry. Since then a number of hilts have been portrayed in other works, namely those of the 6th Dragoon Guards (c.1860), 1st Royal Dragoons (Lieutenant Kempson, 1863) and the 4th Hussars (c.1860). It is also well known that the Royal Engineers adopted the Scroll hilt for their officers, although in this case the guard was manufactured from white metal or monel to minimize corrosion in adverse environmental conditions. In the Cavalry, and Yeomanry Cavalry, the Scroll hilts have been used with a superimposed regimental motif or cipher, for example the 6th Dragoon Guards motif, of the numeral 6 with a surround of crossed carbines, is displayed prominently on the guard, although the various dress regulations generally did not allow for any form of regimental decoration to either blade or hilt.

It is possible then that some cavalry regiments used the Scroll hilt as a means of setting themselves aside from the others in the same manner as the Household Cavalry adopted its own State Swords for each of its three regiments, but retained use of the Regulation Pattern of the time purely as the Service Sword in the field. The presentation of the acanthus decoration has varied over a period of time, from an open cut-out sharp foliage to a broad leafed less fretted form, which may be observed in the five further examples of this rather neglected but purely British cavalry officers' hilt.

87

EIC Scroll hilt.

Illustration 87

This is the guard of the sword for a cavalry officer in the East India Company (EIC), manufactured by Henry Wilkinson, but un-numbered. The rusted and worn condition is a good example of why the Engineers adopted white metal or monel to counter adverse weather. The scrolling foliage is of an open form, the foliage sharp and the cutouts relatively large and covering the whole of the $^1/_2$ basket guard. The general style of the sword is representative of the 1821 pattern Heavy Cavalry Officers' sword. For the sword shown the blade is slightly curved, fullered, and has four embossed panels:

• The EIC Lion holding a Crown, within foliage.
• Crown and VR, within foliage.
• An Arabic script.
• The officer's family crest of a winged horse and a lynx, with the motto: *Virtus Tutissima Cassis*

Blade length	35.43in (90cm)
Sword weight	72lb 3oz (0.98kg)

The author has a photo of a pipe backed sword bearing a Queen Victoria cipher on the blade, with exactly the same sharp cut-out scroll design to the basket guard, putting that sword between the dates 1830 to 1850. The use of the Scroll hilt before its introduction into the 1857 regulations would not be unusual in the history of dress regulations and regulations patterns, there generally being a few years leeway either side of the date. If there had been an abundance of scroll hilted swords around before 1857 then this would have given reasonable cause to introduce the pattern – but only if.

Illustrations 88 (i) & (ii)

This is the sword of Lieutenant C. H. Kempson of the 1st Royal Dragoon's, already described by Brian Robson in the revised edition of *Swords of the British Army*, 1996. This sword is unique in the British Cavalry service and the product of a very individualistic approach to cavalry sword design and disregard to the existing regulation patterns.

It was purchased from Henry Wilkinson's on 5 March 1863, and given the reference number 12378. The purchase receipt is very informative in that on 18 March 1863 it was mounted with the 'New Pattern Hilt Cavalry' (which can only relate to the 1857 dress regulations and the Scroll hilt). The scroll pattern is confined to the lower part of the bowl and is mirror-imaged about the blade and with two sword knot slots towards the rear of the guard. The scrolls are less angular, more rounded and broader leafed than the EIC form. There are three main areas of deviation from the existing 1821 Heavy Cavalry Officers' pattern which would have been current for the 1st Royal Dragoons at the time Kempson purchased this sword:

Conventional view of hilt

88

(i) A shallow bowl guard with broad knucklebow, both equally distributed about the blade and grip; two slots towards the rear of the bowl as an alternative to the more conventional single slot for sword knots at the top of the knucklebow. (It may have been known in 1863 that the new 1864 Pattern Troopers sword was in process of being produced with a bowl guard and identical positions for sword knot, Kempson taking the opportunity to emulate the same condition).

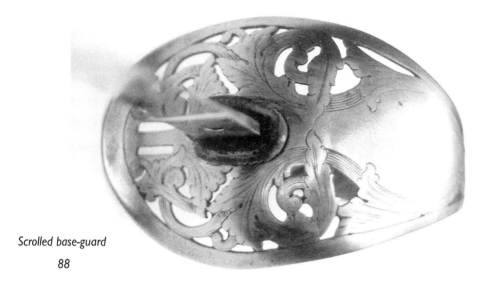

Scrolled base-guard

88

(ii) The pommel is helmet shaped with an extended tail guard, but no integral backstrap to retain the grip. The grip, however, is conventionally covered in fish skin and bound with silver wire. (The only comparison of pommel similarity that can be made is to the style adopted by officers of the 4th Dragoon Guards between 1848 and 1864 and the French Dragoon and Cuirassier swords of 1802 – 1815).

(iii) The blade has a shallow wedge cross-section devoid of decoration, except for the manufacturer's details and an embellished panel with the officer's family crest of a lion guardant and the initials 'CHK'. (Dress Regulations allowed only for inclusion of the Royal Cipher on the blade, although other decoration such as officers' names, initials and regimental motifs when included, as they generally were, were 'acceptable identifications', whereas the absence of the Royal Cipher might be considered by some regiments as discourteous). There is one area that may be contentious. Why was a plain area left on the front of the guard? Was there an intention to add a Regimental Motif in the manner of the Household Cavalry State swords of 1863 and the Shropshire Yeomanry Cavalry hilt shown in Illustration 91. Alas, we may never know that intention for Lieutenant Kempson, who had exchanged to the 1st Royal Dragoons from the 7th Fusiliers in 1862, left his cavalry regiment on 31 March 1863.

Blade length	34.5in (87.5cm)
False Edge length	13.02 (33.0cm)
Sword weight	1lb 1oz (0.93kg)

Scroll hilted sword of Charles Hyde Villiers – Royal Horse Guards Illustration 89

Shows the service sword of Charles Hyde Villiers, who was selected to serve in the Royal Horse Guards in 1887. The sword was purchased from Wilkinsons and numbered 29419. The receipt records two definitive statements regarding the type of hilt; first that it had a patent tang, and secondly that it was a 'Scroll Cav'. This latter clearly again differentiates it from the honeysuckle hilt of the 1821 Heavy Cavalry pattern, and the 1887 Universal Officers' Pattern which was about to evolve. The Household Cavalry Museum is categorical that Villiers' scroll hilted sword was his service sword by preference, and non-regulation as far as his regiment was concerned. The scroll design covers the whole of the 1/2 basket guard in broad leafed foliage etched to give it depth and cutouts to define the outlines.

The pommel and backstrap are diced to prevent slippage, the grip is also diced in a hard wood bound to the broad tang with a 3-band thin wire. The blade is effectively straight, fullered and tapered with a double edge over the last 12.5in (31.75cm) to give an ideal thrusting blade, but nicely balanced for the cutting action. The blade is unadorned except for the manufacturer's details and a scrolled area containing the name 'C. H. Villiers'. The hilt has residual khaki paint to the inside of the guard and outside of the backstrap indicating service in the Boer War, and possibly before that period.

Scroll hilted sword of Charles Hyde Villiers – Royal Horse Guards

89

Blade length   35in (88.5cm)
Sword weight 2lb 3oz (1.00 kg)

Charles Hyde Villiers proved to be an adventurous, resourceful and out of the ordinary cavalryman. Schooled into military life through Chatham and the Royal Military College, he gained certification appropriate at the time, and some knowledge of French, Arabic and Swahili that was to stand him in good stead during his future career. He joined the Royal Horse

Guards as a Second Lieutenant on 21 December 1887, at that point acquiring his scroll hilted sword as a service sword in preference to the 1821 honeysuckle hilted sword (or 1887 as it would later be). This was possibly the first indication that he was an individualist; the second by having the blade of his sword tempered and ground to a finer degree than normal in anticipation of the work that it would be expected to perform in its service life. Promoted to Lieutenant in 1889, he was seconded three years later into the Unyoro Campaign, a punitive expedition, in support of the Sultan of Zanzibar whose lands and protectorates stretched as far as Lake Rudolph in East Africa, a vast area which at that time was in some turmoil from German and other outside influences and interventions. With the success of the campaign and a short period of 'civil' administration he was honoured with the 'Bright Star of Zanzibar', returning to the regiment in 1894 and a promotion to Captain one month later. However, his career was not to be of a static nature, being seconded for a second time, just three months later, but now into a situation that might have been disastrous for his career; part of the duties of an officer on overseas secondment, particularly in areas of interest would be to discover 'the lie of the land', and perhaps 'to get involved'. His secondment to the Chartered British South African Company, founded and run by Rhodes (as a means of furthering his own commercial interests, political ambitions, and those of the Empire), was the ideal place and time to achieve those two aspects of military intelligence that would be much needed in the event of the threatening war with the Boers. Villiers ultimate involvement in the Jameson Raid, although not recorded in his Regimental history, is not a matter of conjecture, being noted by Elizabeth Longford in her history of 'Jameson's Raid', and confirmed by a photograph of Villiers with Jameson and his surviving officers during the enforced journey on board ship back to Great Britain for the judicial sentencing that the Boers demanded after their capture and imprisonment, and eventual release to the British Government. For his sins Villiers was received back into the Royal Horse Guards with the signal honour of Brevet Major, being confirmed as Major in 1897. With the outbreak of the Boer War in 1899, Villiers with his undoubted knowledge of South Africa, found himself seconded for the third and final time to South Africa, principally to help form the South African Light Horse, one of two yeomanry cavalry regiments being formed from refugee

Uitlanders (British subjects forced out of the Transvaal and other territories) each of about 2,000 men. General Buller, on landing in South Africa to take command of the British Forces, enquiring how these regiments were progressing, was plainly 'disappointed' that his staff officer, who had preceded him, Lieutenant Colonel Charles à Court, had already appointed Villiers as Lieutenant Colonel of the South African Light Horse, as he was aware that Villiers 'had ridden with Jameson in the Raid'. Nevertheless, Villiers is recorded in his Regimental History as being not only Major, second in command of the South African Light Horse, but also as 'employer' of that Regiment, signifying some governmental acceptance of his position and a back-handed compliment against Bullers' slight. It is noticeable that Villiers' other responsibility was that of Intelligence Officer. His service in South Africa was distinguished, being mentioned in dispatches, fighting along the Tugela and into the relief of Ladysmith, where, rather ironically, some of his fellow officers of the raid were 'holed-up' attending to their new commercial interests in South Africa. He returned to Great Britain in 1901 to marry Lady Victoria Alexandrina Innes-Kerr, a daughter of the Duke of Roxburghe, and finally to retire from the Royal Horse Guards in 1903. His military life however was not ended, in that year becoming Hon. Lieutenant Colonel of the City of London Yeomanry (Rough Riders), and a Gentleman-at-Arms in 1907.

Hampshire Yeomanry Scroll.

90

Hampshire Yeomanry Scroll
Illustration 90

This is an officer's sword of the Hampshire Carabiniers, purchased by Captain Noel Partridge from Wilkinsons on 24 April 1900, number 37878. The hilt defines the Regimental motif of a crown over a rose on crossed carbines, superimposed upon a total background of close broad leafed scrolling foliage with minimal cutouts or fretting. The pommel and backstrap are diced but of straight infantry form. The blade is effectively straight, fullered and spear pointed, with embossed panels:

- A Rose and Crossed Carbines with Crown, surmounting a Belt containing 'Hampshire Carabiniers', all above a Yeomanry Laurel.
  - The initials 'N.P.'
  - An intertwined back to back VR with Crown and Yeomanry Laurel.
      Blade length   35.06in (89cm)
      Sword weight 2lb 1oz (0.93kg)

A company of the Hampshire Carabiniers served in the 17th Battalion of the Imperial Yeomanry as part of the Rhodesian Field Force during the Boer War.

Shropshire Yeomanry Scroll hilt Illustration 91

Shows an officer's sword of the Shropshire Yeomanry Cavalry. As with the Lieutenant Kempson sword, the Scroll pattern is confined to the lower section of the guard. The upper front section of the guard defines the regimental motif in brass of three leopards heads above a scrolled SYC. The upper section also has a 'ladder' cut into it in the same manner as for the 1796 pattern Heavy Cavalry officers' sword.

Decoration to the straight blade is limited to foliage and a crowned ERI (Edward Rex Imperateur – Edward VII – 1901 – 1910). There are no manufacturing marks, but the proof insert would indicate that it was produced by Thirkle. This sword may have been produced and held for stock.

91

Blade length   35.8in (91cm)
Sword weight 2lb 6oz (1.09kg)
A presentation sword of this type was sold through Wallis and Wallis (28 April 1993) with a date of 1913, indicating that the Scroll Pattern was still being used at the commencement of the 1912 Pattern. The Shropshire Yeomanry Cavalry supplied a company for the 5th Battalion of the Imperial Yeomanry during the Boer War, contributing to Methuen's Column and to the relief of Mafeking.

Shropshire Yeomanry Scroll hilt.

Chapter 11

THE 1880 SERIES OF RANK AND FILE SWORDS

It was not until a committee was established in 1884 that one is able to follow the meanderings, trials and tribulation that accompany the designing of a new sword. The crux of the problem still lay with the 1864 pattern universal sword which had a very slow take off after its pattern date, some regiments not receiving them at all, and those that did eventually beginning to complain of their handling ability, dress damage, and even blades bending when delivering the cut, and, occasionally of breakage. Such criticisms were spread over a long period of time, their impact not really being felt at the War Office, even though they were slowly beginning to filter through from Afghanistan. The War Office also had a secondary problem of sensitivity with this particular sword in that the 'designer' of the pattern was the Commander-in-Chief himself, and any criticism of the sword was a criticism of His Royal Highness himself. The change in design had been simple enough, a retention of the 1853 blade and a replacement of the 3-Bar hilt with a bowl guard, no re-substantiation being required to approve the pattern, and no difference in the function of the sword. However, when the Artillery complained bitterly that the sword was not handleable and that the edge of the large guard was cutting through the stripe of their trousers, and demanding the reversion back to the 1853 pattern, then a change was granted, albeit approving limited minor modifications that wouldn't interfere too much with the general design.

An initial batch of six were converted from production swords of the 1864 pattern in which the hilt was reduced in size and weight, and the edge of the guard was slightly rounded to decrease the liability towards clothing damage; a second sword knot slot was punched out at the top of the hilt (as in the 1853 pattern), as well as in the curl of the guard 'in order to determine a future preferable position'; the blade was slightly thinned and ground narrower, reducing the blade weight, to achieve a stated balance of the sword at 5.25in along the blade from the hilt. This initial batch was sent to the 11th Hussars and the 5th Dragoon Guards for trials, these swords being preferred to the regulation pattern. A second batch of 100 was then sent to 11th Hussars, 20th Hussars, 6th Dragoons and Royal Artillery for further trials and acceptance. This modified sword was termed 'Experimental Sword Pattern 1880'. The reports back from the regiments now became conflicting, still complaining of handleability and clothing damage, the 11th Hussars now saying they thought the blade should be longer than standard. (35.5in), and the Inspector General of Cavalry suggesting that the weight (2lb 2oz) was 'too heavy for the class of man now being enlisted', and that length was not an advantage, and even further suggesting that this new sword should be issued as a service sword for one year and then reviewed. The Director of Artillery however disagreed with this philosophy as he felt the sword could be satisfactory if it had a further modification to the hilt; a view backed by the superintendent of the Royal Small Arms Factory who advocated that the edge of the guard should be rolled to eliminate scuffing. Following these trials and comments, the superintendent was instructed to produce a limited batch of twenty-four with modified hilt and lightened blade but no change in length; this batch was christened: 'Experimental Sword Pattern 1880 (new) with Modified Form of Hilt,' or as later more simply known as Cavalry Sword 1881 (Experimental). In the event, when the batch was received there was a change of heart, using two swords only of the twenty- four, lightening one by 3oz, and the second being shortened by 2in and lightened by ½ oz, these modifications causing minor changes to the centre of balance down to 5in. Following three months of testing in three regiments (2nd Dragoon Guards, 4th Hussars, and 21st Hussars) the new dimensioned swords were approved for cavalry service sword use; the longer sword for heavy cavalry and the shorter sword for light cavalry, i.e. a return to two different swords although universal in their form, and given the official nomenclature of:

Sword Cavalry Pattern 1882 (Long)
Sword Cavalry Pattern 1882 (Short)

1882 Sword adopted by QOCH.
Illustrations 92i, 92ii, 92iii and 92iv

Shows a sword hilt of the 1882 pattern (short) with a shallow bowl guard of 3 ¹/₄ in width (1864 pattern was just over 4in), the base section with rolled edges that would also stiffen the bowl, a sword knot aperture only at the top of the guard, the knucklebow area with a Maltese cross cut out, and a Regimental identification 'QOCH/97' etched into the centre. The grip is of black chequered leather, pinned about the blade tang in five places, the tang being secured in position by an oval domed 'washer'.

The guard is stamped 'Crown /B/21' in the rear curl and 'Mole' near the blade tang. The slightly curved, single fullered and spear pointed blade is marked 'Mole' and 'Crown/E/12' on the back edge, 'Crown/B/21', 'Arrow/WD' and an obsolete mark on one forté side, with '11/85' on the other. An etched and embossed cartouche bearing the words 'Robert Mole & Sons, Makees, Birmingham' is present on one side of the blade.

92i

1882 Sword adopted by QOCH.

Blade length 33in (83.8cm)
Sword weight 2lb 2.5 oz (0.98kg)

In looks and handling this sword is certainly a vast improvement over the 1864 pattern.

The abbreviation QOCH is the identification for the Queen's Own Cameron Highlanders who adopted this form of sword for their rank and file, their officers using the equivalent officers' cavalry pattern of 1821 honeysuckle hilt, or even the Scroll hilt, as in the Scottish Field Officers' sword.

The 1882 patterns were in force in 1884 when the committee was convened. However, by now there was a build up of some 20,000

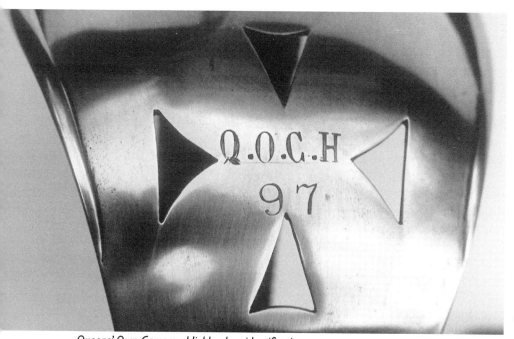

92ii

Queens' Own Cameron Highlanders identification.

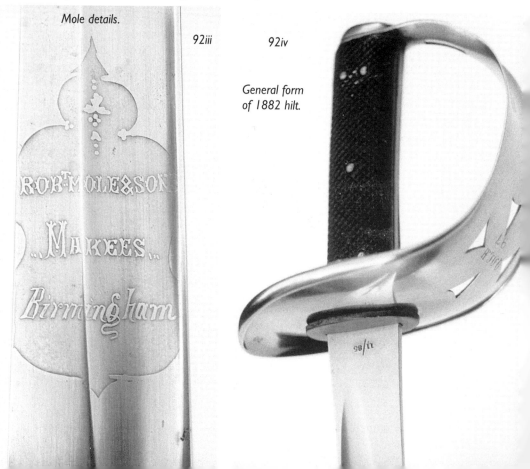

Mole details.

92iii

92iv

General form
of 1882 hilt.

swords in service, in stores, or being made with blades of 1853 and 1864 origin or conversions of one sort or another, and no one knew precisely where or what, some still continuing to bend or break in action, as was being demonstrated by the 10th Hussars, newly returned from India with swords that were noticeably faulty. The first task of the committee was to inspect the swords of the 10th Hussars, and also those of the 16th Lancers who now joined the succession of complaints. The committee was composed of service Cavalry Officers, representatives of the stores departments of Britain and India, the Royal Small Arms Factory, the War Office chemist, a Member of Parliament (presumably to monitor costs and see that it was being spent wisely), one of the blade manufacturers, and was chaired by the Inspector General of Cavalry. The committee therefore was capable of technical input as well as serving experience, their first inspection taking place on 4 November 1884. They were not at all happy with what they saw and heard, their immediate reaction was to suspend all manufacture of the 1882 Patterns at Robert Mole and Sons, Birmingham, on the basis that the new swords were 'not of the best steel, and bend out of shape; this is the case with all the latest issue of swords'.

There were two immediate reactions to this disastrous statement: Mole, who must have had some previous inkling as to how his swords were performing, immediately offered an alternative experimental sword that they had been working on, a sword that was heavier and of different blade form, but which failed when tested by the committee; the committee then instructed that a number of swords of various conversion be taken at random, subject to retesting to the original test specification for striking on edge and back, and, if they passed, to move on to a more stringent series of bend checks of 5in reduction in blade length. Of thirty-five swords tested in this manner, two broke, and two bent on the oak block strike – nearly a 12 per cent failure rate. Also, in the meantime, they requested the Royal Small Arms Factory to produce a small quantity with blade lengths 34in and 34.5in, with Mole supplying a further four of their own accord. Eight of these swords were tested by strike and reduction by $5\frac{1}{2}$in, two failed in bending and one at the strike – a 37 per cent failure rate. With the situation worsening, the committee then recommended that 'the swords of present patterns are not satisfactory, and that the whole of them should be retested to eliminate those that are soft.' Those that are in the hands of the troops to be withdrawn gradually for this purpose. Such as withstand the further test to be reissued'. They further took the precaution of requesting the Royal Small Arms Factory to prepare a specification for swords with blades of 34.5in length. For comparison tests the committee requested that six swords be made to the new specification, and that six of each of the two types of 1882 Pattern be procured and tested generally with a cut at the gallop against carcasses of horses and sheep by serving men of the 1st Life Guard, 15th and 25th Hussars. In practice: five swords of 1882 (Long) were tested; one broke, the other four bent in a total of fifteen cuts; six swords of 1882 (Short) when tested, one fully passed, the other five bent or twisted in a total of nine cuts; six swords with 34in blades (RSAF had been unable to maintain limitation length, weight and balance to maintain 34.5in): one sword broke, one sword slightly bent on its 7th and 8th cuts (an excessive test compared with the others), three bent and the 6th sword passed but on only one cut, a total of fourteen cuts being delivered. In addition a Life Guard sword and a sword with a 33in blade were opportunely tested, both swords bending after two and one cut respectively. These results may be taken as inconclusive as the cuts were delivered in different strengths, and the number per sword were at a variance with each other. The effects of bending and breakage however were of concern to the committee who then decided to consult with the blade suppliers and sword manufacturers. In the event, only Sandersons and Firth of Sheffield, and Mole, attended, the discussions centring around methods of hardening, steel grade and carbon content, which again were conflicting and inconclusive. Sandersons favoured water hardening, whilst Firth favoured oil hardening, with Mole wavering between the two. Sanderson stated that when they had received contracts from Mole they had received no specification, consequently providing a second grade cast steel, and not the best quality they were capable of making. Firth on the other hand had always supplied the finest grade to Wilkinsons with 1.04 per cent carbon content. The committee concluded that they should see some more swords tested, this time four from each supplier (RSAF, Wilkinsons and Moles), two to be water hardened, two to be oil hardened; they also reinforced their original recommendation to withdraw and retest the 1882 pattern swords. The discussions with the suppliers subsequently met with some acrimony, Sanderson recording that the information they had given had subsequently been fed into the public domain and that the committee had breached the confidentiality that was expected of such a meeting; the alleged perpetrator of this indelicacy responding and recording the minutes with 'the incident would not have occurred had there been a technical school in Sheffield', a somewhat unsubtle slight on the lack of technical expertise that was being applied by the suppliers and manufacturers. However, the process to arrive at the crux of the problems experienced over the last twenty years had only taken fifteen months from the formation of the committee in October 1884 to the decisions made at this meeting in January 1886. In the event, and as appeared to be normal, only ten new swords were received for testing, four from Enfield, four from Mole and two from Wilkinson, these in equal quantities of water and oil hardening. Testing procedure was more stringent than before: first to be bent around a rigid metal curve to reduce blade length by 5in; secondly to subject the hilt to a pressure and reduce the blade length by 5in, and then by 6in; by being struck very heavily on an oak block first on the edge and then on the back. Two of the swords to be further bent at 11in, and then re-struck. For Wilkinson, both swords supplied by Firth with 1.04 per cent carbon content, the water hardened blade started to bend even with the first test, getting progressively worse through to the last test of striking on the edge; the oil hardened blade only bent at the edge strike after being passed at a 6in bend. Mole, on the other hand had two swords supplied by Sanderson with 1.2 per cent carbon content, both oil hardened, one of which broke on the edge strike after bending slightly at 6in, but thought to be a flaw in the steel; the second bent on the edge strike, and again on the back strike after a 6in bend. Of the other two blades by Firth, one broke at the edge strike after a 6in bend, the other bent slightly at both strikes and bent further at 11in. For the RSAF Enfield, the two water hardened blades broke when striking on the edge after a 6in bend, one found to be a flaw in the neck join of tang to blade; the two oil hardened blades passed on the procedure through to back strike, one sword bending slightly at 11in, and retaining a degree of bend into the following edge and back strikes.

These results would certainly seem to have given them a case for oil hardening, and to a specification that Enfield would be able to deduce. In May 1885 the committee authorized a new pattern sword from this specification, the 1885 Pattern Cavalry Sword for rank and file. To arrive at the 1885 Pattern a number of changes had been made to the previous sword form, whether arising from the criticisms of the troops who used them, or from the observations of the committee. The blade length had now been established at 34.5in, once again a universal sword for both heavy and light cavalry, and with a sword weight of 2lb 5oz, the point of balance hovering around the 5in to 5¹/₄in mark, much dependent on manufacturing tolerances. To ease a complaint that the hilt hurt the edge of the hand, a formed convex curved metal 'pad' was fitted at the join of the top of the guard with the grip; the sword knot aperture was re-established at the top of the guard; the rolled edge of the guard became more prominently rolled. During this process a large number of swords had been made anew to suit a particular purpose, or for experiment, or converted from one pattern to another, some even going through several experimental stages, some experimental swords being termed 'service swords' for operational testing, some rejected at the initial mechanical checks, some being rejected through flaws found in the modification process. Such a sword is shown in **Illustration 93i and 93ii.**

This sword demonstrates the general characteristics of the 1885 Pattern, but also some of the earlier conversions. The pommel is flattened, not rounded off as in the production version, and stamped with a testing reference number '5/1B'. There are two sword knot apertures as in the 1864 and the Experimental 1880/81 swords, and the incorporated 'pad' of the ultimate 1885. The blade length is

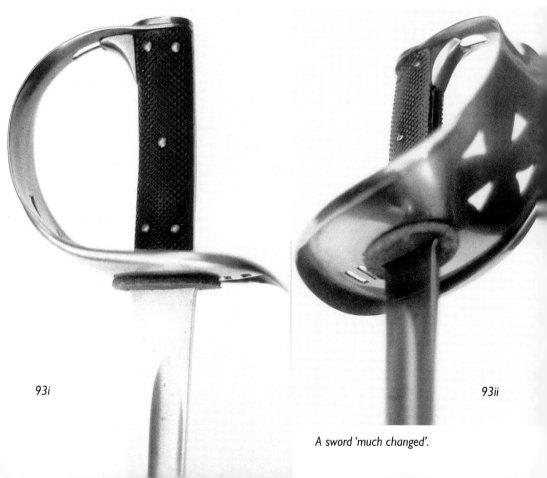

93i

93ii

A sword 'much changed'.

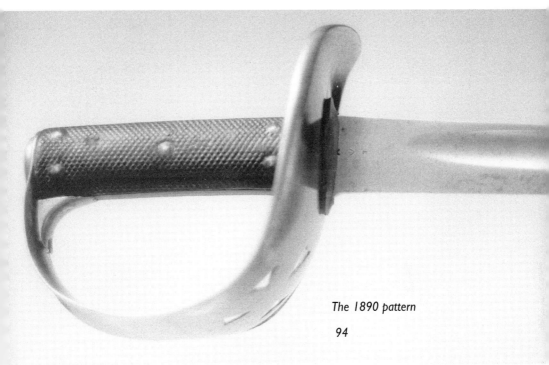

The 1890 pattern

94

34.5in with a point of balance of 5 $\frac{1}{4}$ in and a sword weight of 2lb 4$\frac{1}{2}$ oz. There are no manufacturers markings on the blade, but during the blade thinning process a distinct flaw of 4$\frac{1}{2}$in was discovered in the material grain.

The 1885 pattern continued through to 1889, at that date a few minor changes taking place to both blade and guard to improve its handleability, to give first the Experimental Pattern 1889, ultimately becoming the 1890 Pattern Cavalry Sword. An example of this is shown in **Illustration 94** in which the Pattern Date '/ 90' is stamped on the back edge of the blade, with various viewing marks on one forté side, and issue dates '95 through to '04 on the other.

Also in 1889 the War Office conducted a comparison between British and foreign cavalry swords, with the 1885, 1889 Exp, and the Household Cavalry Patterns 1882 and 1888 as the base for comparison, and twenty-three from France, Germany, Austria, Italy, Egypt, Spain and Russia, using weight, blade length, reduction, balance, fullered section, blade width and thickness as the factors of comparison.

The report is not conclusive, other that that the four British swords were placed top in order of merit: (1) 1882 H/C (2) 1888 H/C (3) 1885 (4) 1889 Exp. This did not prevent the War Office from

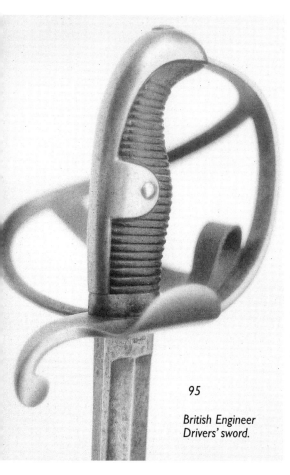

95

*British Engineer
Drivers' sword.*

ultimately contracting for what the Enfield Pattern Room called 'German, Sword Cavalry Universal, 1889 Pattern' for use by some British Mounted Troops, notably for Engineer Drivers, as in **Illustration 95**.

An unidentified German sabre, of heavy weight construction with wide, thick curved blade, etched 'P.Knecht in Solingen' with British Crown and obsolete markings may also have been tested but found unsuitable though the factors of blade length 32.75in, sword weight 2lb 8oz, and a point of balance of $6^1/_2$in, contrary to the committee findings. This sword is shown in **Illustration 96**.

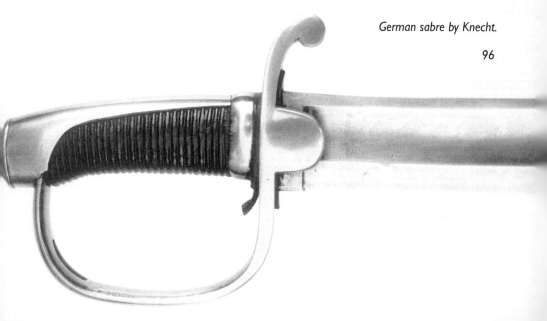

German sabre by Knecht.

96

Chapter 12

RANK AND FILE SWORDS
FROM 1890 TO 1908

Despite the preceding ten years of development and the actions taken by the committee formed in 1884, the 1890 pattern was by no means perfect. Considerable effort was still taking place and would be for the next twenty years in pursuit of what the experts would eventually consider to be the ideal sword for the cavalry. The rank and file, however, were to have little input into its development, unlike the officers who had the ability to determine the form or type of weapon they could use in service (witness Kempson, Villiers, and that unknown patriot of Illustration 73). The criticisms of bending and breaking were to continue, even into the Boer War, and the next pattern, the 1899 was not to correct those deficiencies, or any other.

The 1899 pattern for rank and file
Illustration 97

The blade for this new pattern sword was similar to the 1890, but the centre of balance was decreased to 4in out from the guard, making the sword hilt-heavy. At a total weight for the sword of 2lb 11oz (1.23kg), the handleability of the sword in action became more limited and handling time durability was decreased. The difference in centre of balance position was due to the form and weight of the new hilt. Following the same principle of the tang being the basis of the grip since 1853, both tang and grip had now been extended to 6in, a length increase which allowed the hand to slip over the grip by up to 2in, which was not conducive to good control in the heat of action or to control the additional weight of the extended guard. The chequered leather grips were retained about the tang by three pins secured over washers.

The convexed corner pad between grip and the inside top of the guard was retained from the 1885-90 patterns to prevent damage to the back of the hand. The guard is of heavy plate with a rear curl, forming a shallow bowl whose edges may have been rounded, but many examples do not show this characteristic to advantage. Many examples show that the guard edge could be subject to damage and burring. The guard

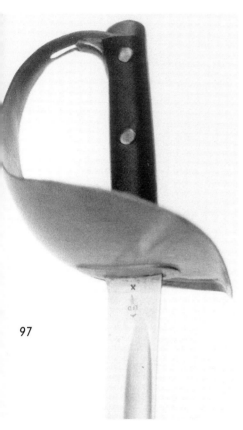

97

1899 Pattern Troopers' sword.

is reinforced at the blade entry with a broad pear shaped plate also of heavy construction. **Illustration 97** shows a typical example of this pattern. The blade is slightly curved, single fullered and 33.5in long (85cm), and has a number of markings.

Back edge: (Pattern) '/99; Crown/20/E.

Outer Forté: Arrow; 'EFD' (For Enfield Small Arms Factory); obsolete mark.

Inner Forté: Issue marks for '01,'04, '05, '06, '07, and '08.

Viewing marks: Crown/F6/E; Crown/U8/E; Crown/34/E.

The guard has residual khaki paint, the rear curl stamped with '10.03' and two Regimental markings: 3/DG/316 and F.K.Y/160. These indicate that the sword was primarily in service with the 3rd Dragoon Guards, and then passed to the Fife & Kinross Yeomanry to complete its service life until the substitution of the 1908 Pattern.

The 3rd Dragoon Guards (also known as the 3rd Carabiniers) served in the Boer War from 1899 through to 1902, gaining distinction at the Relief of Kimberley and the Battle of Paardeberg. The 3rd Dragoon Guards also had the unusual distinction of being one of the few cavalry regiments to go into action with its front rank using lances to carry out an initial ground clearing action, the second rank bearing only carbines, and the third rank using both carbines and swords.

This unusual tactic was apparently a legacy from their time in India, and the Indian Mutiny, and subsequent small wars against irregular forces 'when the lance was found to be a handy weapon against men lying on the ground, especially in the undergrowth', which seemed to be a good way of dealing with hidden subversives and guerrillas, and particularly relevant to these aspects of the Boer War.

Sword of the 2nd County of London Yeomanry (Westminster Dragoons) c. 1900
Illustration 98

This sword appears to have been modelled upon the Infantry officers' 1897 pattern and was peculiar to the 2nd CLY However, the guard is plain without any form of decoration and the grip material has been changed to a black polished composite. For the sword as illustrated, the combined pommel backstrap has the entire length of the backstrap chequered, the semi ovoid pommel has a single line decoration and the grip is ribbed without wire binding, both grip and backstrap are secured at the guard with a ribbed ferrule.

The sheet metal guard takes the same form as the infantry sword but is entire and plain, with a sword knot aperture at the top curve. The inside of the guard retains a layer of old khaki paint. The blade is straight, rectangular in cross section at the forté, leading into a central single fullered length of 11.5in, the remainder of the blade profiling into a shallow wedge section and

98

Sword of the 2nd County of London Yeomanry (Westminster Dragoons) c. 1900.

tapering into a thrusting spear point. The actual thrusting capability of this sword may have been put into debate as the last 19in of the blade could be termed 'flexible'. At the blade forté the supplier details are shown as 'Hamburger, Rogers & Co., London'. Both officers and other ranks used the same pattern sword.

Blade length	34.5in (87cm)
Sword weight	2lb (0.9kg)

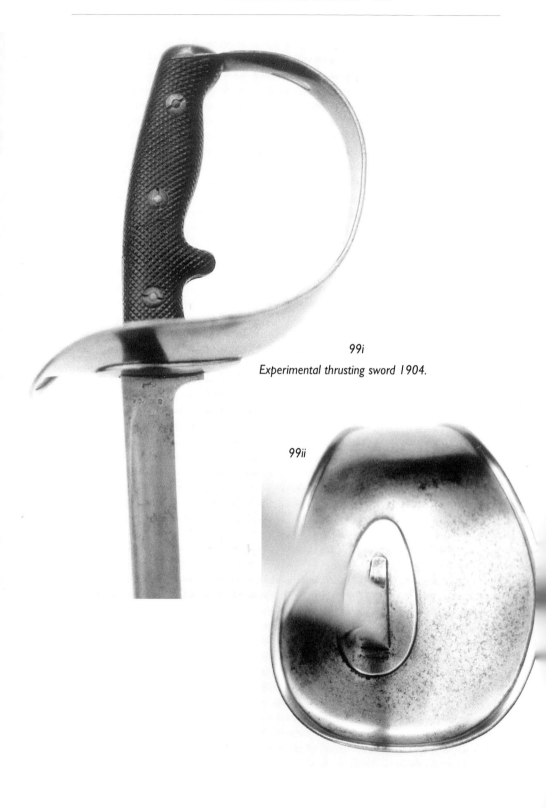

99i
Experimental thrusting sword 1904.

99ii

The 2nd County of London Yeomanry sword with its straight part stiff blade shows the growing trend of adaptation towards the thrusting sword. This trend was also in the minds of the War Department as a form of sword to be developed purely for cavalry, progressively pursuing its research and tests around blades which possessed strength in their cross section, and gradually reducing or eliminating the cutting edge, and adapting the grip so that the thumb, forefinger and hand could reinforce the thrusting action by the use of 'pistol grips'. Whilst a number of these 'thruster' forms were produced and tested, the first most successful was that produced in 1904 and called the Experimental 1904 Pattern Cavalry Sword, a number of which were put into service. A typical example of this pattern is shown in Illustrations 99 (i) & (ii) which clearly show the form of the pistol grip.

The other significant feature of this sword is that the blade cross-section is in the form of a 'T'. The grip still employed the principle of being based on the blade tang, shaped from $^5/_{16}$in thick steel, with chequered area at the thumb enforcement point, with two shaped wooden chequered grip pads screwed across the tang by three pins that could be secured or removed by a simple screwdriver. The grip was shaped to enable the forefinger to curl around the 'trigger', limiting slide and allowing the force of the hand and arm to be directed into the thrust. The guard was a shallow bowl with small rolled edges finishing at the rear curl, and reinforced by a pear shaped plate at the blade entry point. The blade is straight, tapering into a shallow spear point, the 'T' section running to within 6in of the point. The back edge is stamped: (Pattern) '04; and 'EFD'. Forté sides marked

i) '8'; '04; Crown/75/E

ii) Arrow; Crown/75/E; Obsolete

As a thrusting sword, as it was intended, it is much stiffer and less flexible than the 2nd CLY sword, and an obvious progression towards what many people have termed the ultimate sword.

Blade length	35in (88.8cm)
Sword weight	2lb 2oz (0.95kg)

It took another four years of experimentation and tests to evolve the 'ultimate' cavalry sword, and even then in two stages, the 1908 pattern Calvalry sword Mks I & II.

Illustrations 100 (i) & (ii) show a typical example of the Mk II, which in every way is different from the 1904 pattern, with the 1908 Mk I differing only in minor changes in grip material and shape. The grip is formed and shaped to the hand from a hard rubber brick-red composite six inches long through which the blade tang is secured by a domed pommel. There is a chequered thumb 'push' on the outer edge, the hand grip area being only 3 ^{3}/$_4$ in between raised sections preventing hand slippage. The guard is a large bowl with rear curl and rolled edges, the base of the guard reinforced with an extended 'pear drop' plate. The blade is straight, the major part of a blunt edged wedged section, fullered and tapering into a shallow spear point, the last eight inches being double edged, but not capable of cutting. The marking on the blade is:

Back edge: P'08

Forté Sides: a) Arrow; Crown/75/E; Obsolete mark

b) '13'; '15; '18; Crown/75/E; Crown/7A/E

On the guard the following marks are apparent: Arrow; 'WSC' (Wilkinson Sword Company); Crown/J1/E'. A regimental identification 'ID' has been cut out on the outer edge of the grip (1st Royal Dragoons).

<table>
<tr><td>Blade length</td><td>35.18in (89.4cm)</td></tr>
<tr><td>Sword weight</td><td>3lb (1.35kg)</td></tr>
</table>

The 1st Royal Dragoons were still in South Africa when the First World War broke out, taking them just three months to ship back to Great Britain, re-form as part of the 3rd Cavalry Division, and ship out to Belgium in early October 1914, engaging the Germans at Ypres on the 14th, and another 'sharp encounter' at Kemmel the same day with 'C' Squadron gaining the advantage, using the same horses they had used in South Africa. Thereafter they met up with the machine gun and improvised German armoured cars, which forced them into trench warfare. However, they did have some other 'cavalry' success, holding the fort against immeasurable odds at Zandvoorde, and engaging the Germans at Neuve Chapelle and Loos in 1915, Arras in 1917, and 'dragoon' activity at Collezy, and Hamel in 1918, with a final successful cavalry charge at Le Cateau contributing towards 450 prisoners, ten guns, and over fifty machine guns that were taken

1908 Pattern of the 1st Royal Dragoons   *100i*

100ii

and the rout of the Germans in general. So all was not lost for the cavalry, but there was also a general recognition that times were changing, and the sword was no longer a weapon that could be used to any effect in modern warfare.

The 1908 Indian Troopers' Sword

This troopers' sword was a direct development from the 1908 regulation pattern but adapted specifically for use in India. The bowl guard hilt was much lighter, more shallow and without decoration; the pommel was of the domed form, but smaller and lighter, and the grip in chequered wood. The blade was of the same basic form as the 1908, but shorter in length.

Illustrations 101i, 101ii and 101iii

This is a regimental variation with 1908-1912 derivations, and adapted for Indian use of the 33rd Light Cavalry. The grip is of the general form of the 1908, a trifle smaller and carved in wood, with a thumb depression on the outer edge, the two sides each with a chequered diamond. The bowl guard has its edges rolled, leading into a rear curl. The guard is stamped '33.L.C' on the outside surface towards the rear curl. The blade is adapted from

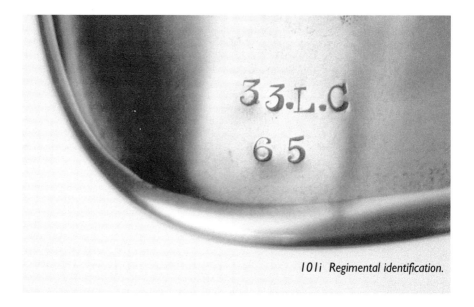

101i Regimental identification.

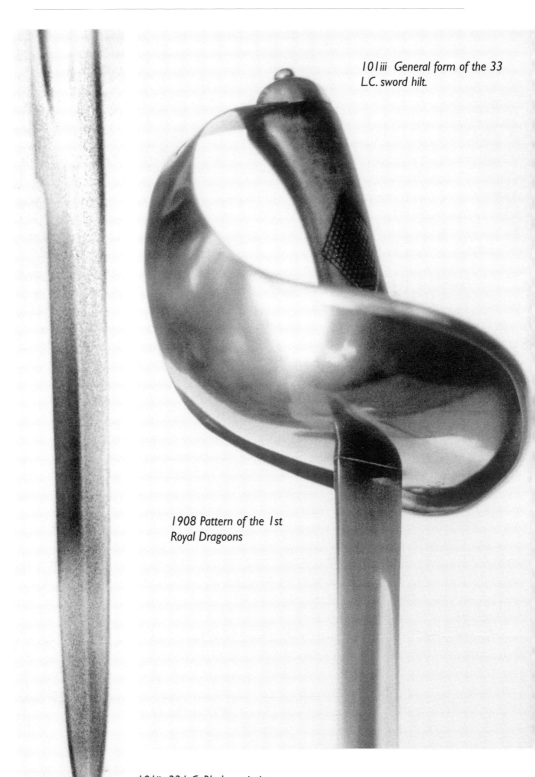

101iii *General form of the 33 L.C. sword hilt.*

1908 Pattern of the 1st Royal Dragoons

101ii *33.L.C. Blade variation.*

a slightly curved fullered form in which the back edge has been cut away over the last 9in to make a near double-edged thrusting point. The forté is stamped 'Wilkinson', with an obsolete mark.

Blade length	34.75in (88.25cm)
Sword weight	2lb 4oz (0.99kg)

The officers' version is identical to this troopers' sword in its form, but the outside of the guard is etched with the broad honeysuckle motif of the 1912 pattern officers' sword, and the blade etched with the cipher of the 33rd Light Cavalry.

Chapter 13

OFFICERS' SWORDS AFTER THE 1821 PATTERNS THROUGH TO 1912

Whilst there had been a considerable number of changes to the rank and file swords from 1821 in both Light and Heavy cavalry, and there had been a progression into universal swords for both arms, the Officers' sword had remained reasonably static through to 1887. Individual officers however had taken opportunities to equip themselves with swords to their own liking, but in general stayed with either the 3-Bar or honeysuckle hilt according to whichever division of the cavalry they were in. There were a few exceptions where Regiments adopted the 1857 Scroll hilt in addition to the regulation pattern, and there was also the specific case of the 4th Dragoon Guards officers who adopted a variation to the honeysuckle hilt whereby the guard was considerably extended, the pommels resembling the 'helmets' of the French models AN.XI and AN.XII, but in steel, and the blades being modelled upon the 2nd L.G and RHG Officers' state swords of 1832. The 4th/7th Dragoon Guards Museum in York has two examples of these swords, one dated 1848 and the other 1864. Both these swords bear decoration on the blades, the hilts in steel, but one hilt has some gilt decoration. A

4th Dragoon Guards special pattern.
102i

further example of this variation is shown in **Illustrations 102 (i) & (ii):**

The outward extension of the guard can be seen quite clearly. The width of the guard is 5in, as opposed to a normal width of 4in. The inner edge is curled upwards, and the rear edge is curled drastically downwards. The base of the guard around the blade is left clear of honeysuckle decoration, but for the rest of the guard the honeysuckle cutouts follow the pattern laid out for the 1821 heavy cavalry sword. The distinctive 'helmet' pommel (similar to some of the French Dragoon Swords) surmounts a blackened fish skin grip bound in silver wire. The blade is heavy, straight, single fullered with shallow hatchet point, designed for thrusting. The forté bears the manufacturers details: 'F.I (for J) Cater, 156 Pall Mall, London', which would put the date of the blade between 1832 and 1839. This presumably meant that it had been re-hilted at some later date. Both sides of the blade are decorated with a single panel of 'Crown with sunrays, VR, and Laurel Wreath', one side only with a partly obliterated family crest, one part appearing to be a swan, the second part in which a crown is distinguishable above a castellated tower.

102ii

4th Dragoon Guards special pattern.

Blade length	38in (96.5cm)
Sword weight	2lb 5oz (1.05kg)

In 1880 there were moves, along with the changes being made to the rank and file swords to make some changes to the officers' swords. These changes however were limited and not undertaken.

Experimental officers sword c. 1881
Illustrations 103i and 103ii

This shows one of these experimental swords in which the grip, pommel backstrap are based upon the 1821 patterns, but the guard has now become a sheet metal bowl, the outer periphery with line decoration, and the base with eight circular and one forward central ovoid cut outs

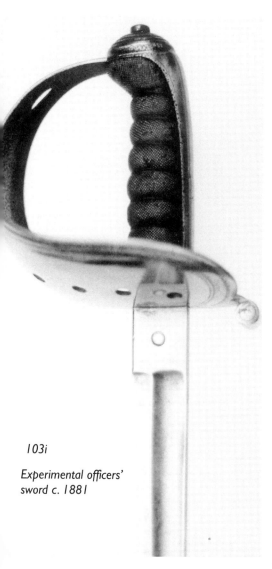

103i

*Experimental officers'
sword c. 1881*

in the style of the Austrian cavalry sabre of 1869. The blade is in effect straight, single fullered and spear pointed, devoid of decoration, but with a plain brass proof insert.
Blade length   35in (88.8cm)
Sword weight 2lb2oz (0.98kg)

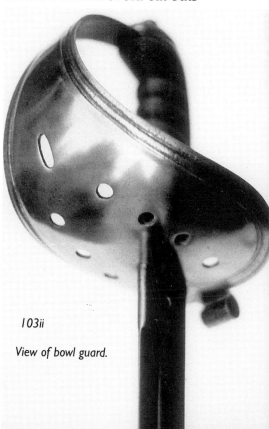

103ii

View of bowl guard.

In 1887 a universal pattern sword was introduced for both heavy and light cavalry officers. This sword was not far removed from the existing 1821 heavy cavalry officers' sword with fullered blade and honeysuckle hilt, the differences being that the blade was in effect straight, and of heavier section than the 1880 Experimental of Illustration 103, the pommel backstrap followed the straight form of the infantry swords of the time, and the honeysuckle guard was of heavier plate.

1887 pattern – 4th Hussars.

104ii

104i

1887 pattern – 4th Hussars
Illustrations 104i and 104ii

Show a sword of the 4th Hussars to this standard form. The pommel backstrap is chequered overall. The blade shows the sword to have been supplied by 'Hamburger Rogers & Co, King Street, London, W6', and has decoration on both sides:
i) Crown under sunrays; VR; foliage.
ii) Foliage; 4th Hussars /Crown/VR; foliage.
The back edge is stamped with the number 4971, and the sword is plated overall.
Blade length   36.25in (92cm)
Sword weight   2lb 4oz (1.03kg)

1887 Indian pattern
Illustrations 105i and 105ii

Show an 1887 pattern sword specifically adapted for Indian service. The pommel back-strap is plain except for some striations in the area of the thumb rest. The grip is fish skin covered, bound in copper wire. The guard is broader than normal at 4³/₄in and is spread equi-distantly about the grip with cutouts to represent the honeysuckle decoration but without line decoration. The blade, by 'Thurkle, London' is slightly curved for cutting, rather than thrusting, and bears a silvered proof insert. The blade is decorated on both sides, and marked:

i) Outer Forté: 'ISD' (Indian Stores Dept); Arrow; 'I'.
ii) Back edge: 'London Made'.
iii)Foliage; Crown with sunrays/VRI/a small representation of embossed and inter-twined clover leaf, rose and thistle
iv) Repeated on other side.

Blade length   32.5in (82.5cm)
Sword weight 2lb (0.9kg)

105i

1887 Indian pattern.

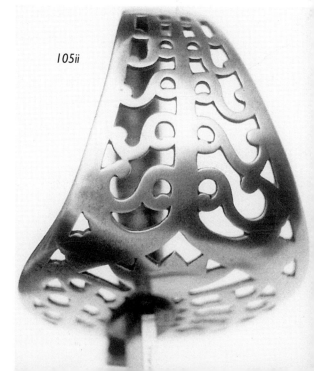

105ii

No further development was undertaken for officers' swords until the changes of 1904 and 1908, for those of rank and file had been effected and proved. After 1908 the Officers' pattern of 1912 was evolved, taking into account the minor changes of the 1908, and the necessity to allow for some differentiation in distinguishing the Officers from the Rank and File, otherwise the two swords were of identical form.

1912 Officers Pattern.

106

1912 Officers' pattern   Illustration 106

This shows the standard regulation form. The pommel is stepped with foliage decoration. The grip is blackened fish skin covered with silver wire binding. The broad bowl guard is decorated with a broad interpretation of the honeysuckle pattern (which by now had been in continuous existence on British Cavalry swords since 1821, and intermittently before then). The blade follows the 1908 form, but in this case gives the supplier details; 'Bartles & Co, Hanover Court, Hanover St' and has decoration on both sides:
i)Foliage; Crown/ sunrays /Royal Coat of Arms/G.V.R/Laurel Wreath/Foliage.
ii) Foliage; Crossed Lances behind Skull and Cross Bones/17/'Or Glory' (17th Lancers); Laurel Wreath; Foliage.

Blade length	33.5in (90.2cm)
Sword weight	2lb 3oz (1.98kg)

Indian 1912 regulation pattern for officers
Illustration 107

This pattern sword is basic-ally to the form of the 1908 Rank and File regulation pattern for India, but has the refinements of the 1912 to distinguish it as an Officers' sword. **Illustration 107** shows the modified grip as tapering from the pommel down to the thumb rest on the outer edge and the forefinger rest on the inner edge, and is fish skin covered, with silver wire binding. The pommel, in steel, is ovoid but squared off, with no steps or foliage decoration as in the regulation of 1912. The guard is decorated with the broad honeysuckle pat-tern about a frontal classical shield containing a 'GRI' scroll. The blade is of the 1908 form, invariably stamped 'P. '08' on the back edge and 35in in length.

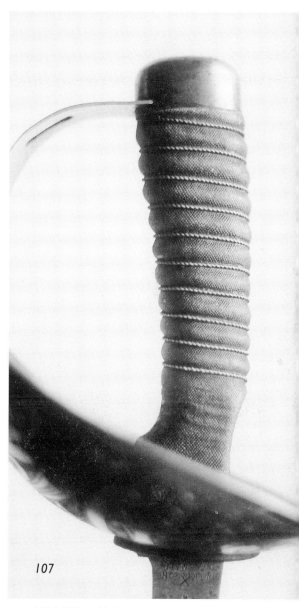

107

1912 Officers' Indian pattern

1912 variation   Illustrations 108i and 108ii

Show a Shropshire Yeomanry Officers' sword probably with a family blade of 1887 form re-hilted with a 1912 hilt. The hilt is in white metal, the honeysuckle in a raised form to accentuate the design, the stepped pommel being chequered over the flat top following re-hilting. The grip is blackened fish skin covered, bound with silver wire. The blade is in effect straight, single fullered and supplied by 'Austin & Oaker, Conduit Street, London', numbered '99380' and decorated both sides:

i) Foliage; Crown with sunrays; VR; Foliage.

ii) Foliage; 'Shropshire'/Crossed be-ribboned Lances/'Yeomanry'; Foliage.

Blade length	35.87in (91.2cm)
Sword weight	2lb 2oz (1.25kg)

1912 Yeomanry variant

108i

108i

Chapter 14

HOUSEHOLD CAVALRY SWORDS FROM 1832 TO 1912

In 1832 the Household Cavalry Officers had adopted three standard forms of dress or state swords, quite spectacular compared with the swords of the Light and Heavy Cavalries, and which deserve special mention and description.

1st Life Guards c. 1832 Illustrations 109i and 109ii

Show the Officers' state sword of the 1st Life Guards from 1832 to 1872. The pommel backstrap is built up from a stepped pommel in brass, and a backstrap of smoothed steel. The grip is fish skin covered and bound in brass wire. The guard is of a shallow bowl in steel with a lined peripheral edge pinned with twelve brass studs. At the top of the guard is a sword knot aperture and a cutout ladder, similar to that employed on the 1796 Heavy Cavalry Officers' sword. The front of the guard has a series of cut outs coincident with a raised crown over '1' and a scrolled cipher 'L.G', both in brass and pinned through the guard. The blade is plain, straight, of heavy fullered section, leading into a spear point, and intended for thrusting, if it was used in action.

Blade length   37.75in (95.8cm)
Sword weight   2lb 6oz (1.1kg)

This particular sword is ex-Sheffield Park, through Wallis & Wallis sale 27 April 1971.

1st Life Guards c. 1832

109i   *109ii*

2nd Life Guards' State sword c.1832 Illustrations 110i and 110ii

This is a typical officers' state sword of the 2nd Life Guards from 1832 to 1872. This form of sword is modelled upon the French cuirassier swords, but anglicized into a more dramatic and acceptable form for the Household Cavalry purposes of their ceremonial duties. The pommel is distinctive in its brass 'helmet' form, with a backstrap depicting a flaming grenade within wings and bolts of lightning. The grip is formed, fish skin covered and bound in brass wire. The guard is of a 4-Bar form with interconnecting scrolled bars, probably adapted from the plainer 4-Bar hilt of the French AN XI and XIII Models. The base guard has representations of the flaming grenade on both inner and outer surfaces, the origins of this motif arising from the regiment's Grenadier Guards function. The blade is straight, single fullered, and tapers to a shallow hatchet point, and was supplied by 'Andrews, 9 Pall Mall' (probably 1821 to 1825), and decorated on both sides:

A wreath, of acorns and oak leaves to one side (refer to

2nd Life Guards' State sword c.1832.

110i

Chapter 2, Illustrations 17 & 18) and palms on the other side; Regimental insignia of a scrolled 2 L.G; a flaming grenade; a crown.
Blade length 38.25in(97.2cm)
Sword weight 2lb 6oz (1.1kg)

110ii

Winged grenade and lightning pommel.

Royal Horse Guards' State sword c. 1832 Illustration 111i and 111iii

This is the state sword for officers of the Royal Horse Guards from 1832 to 1872. This sword utilizes the same brass 4-Bar hilt form as for the 2nd Life Guards, but the pommel is cast with honeysuckle fronds about a single rose; the base guard is cast on the inner and outer surfaces with a crown. This particular sword is distinguished by having the Flintshire family of Hanmer crest of a lion guardant on a baronets chapeau etched onto the inner face of the knucklebow and a matching crest on the scabbard. The grip is fish skin covered and bound with a 3-rope brass wire. The blade is straight, single fullered, and tapering to a shallow hatchet point. The blade has no decoration, and was supplied by 'Prosser, Manufacturers to the King, Charing Cross' which would indicate the blade was manufactured in the broad range 1797 to 1853, and further certified by a Prosser proof mark.

Blade length	39.37in (100cm)
Sword weight	2lb 6oz (1.1kg)

The Household Cavalry Museum has confirmed that there were two members of the Hanmer family who could have carried this sword: a) Henry Hanmer, who joined the RHG in 1808, and served in the Peninsular Campaign from 1812 to 1814, participating in the battles of Vittoria and Pamplona in 1813, retiring as Major in December 1832. b) Edward Wyndham Hanmer (later Sir Edward) who served in the RHG from 1829, receiving Brevet Major in 1846, and transferring to the 6th Iniskilling Dragoons in 1849.

Royal Horse Guards' State Sword c. 1832.

111i

Rose and scroll pommel

111ii

In 1872 the three Regiments of the Household Cavalry changed to a common presentation for their state swords, based upon the 1832 form of the 1st Life Guards as shown in Illustration 108, but with different ciphers for each regiment, the 1st Life Guards retaining its original scrolled cipher. Although some transient forms became apparent, and 'period' changes (such as blade cross section as in the case of swords for the reign of Queen Elizabeth II), this common form has remained in existence until present time.

2nd Life Guards' transitional form 1860 – 1883
Whilst the guard was changed to the steel bowl with twelve studded periphery and crown with scrolling 2.L.G. in brass, the pommel reflected the transition in which the top became domed and chequered in brass; the remainder in polished steel. A sword of this form was carried by Lieutenant Colonel George A. Curzon from 1860 to 1888.

2nd Life Guards' State sword, 1872 to 1883
Illustrations 112i and 112ii

The regimental cipher '2 L.G.' is presented as a symmetrical scrolled 'LG.GL/2' in brass and pinned to the guard. In some cases the cipher is removable to allow cleaning both guard area and cipher as separate items. The pommel is domed, the upper half in brass, the backstrap in steel. For the sword illustrated, the supplier was 'Hawkes & Co, London, Manufacturers to the Queen', putting the date between 1853 and 1890. The proof mark is by Reeves. The blade is straight, single fullered and spear pointed, without any identification.

Blade length	36.25in (92.1cm)
Sword weight	2lb 1oz (0.93kg)

Royal Horse Guards' State sword, 1872 to 1883
Illustrations 113i and 113ii

The essential difference here is only the Royal Horse Guards' cipher, which is scrolled in brass of irregular form, and pinned to or removable from the guard. The sword, by 'Henry Wilkinson, Pall Mall, London', is numbered, but believed to be what is termed a 'stock' sword for general issue to officers and normally held in store when not in use. The blade is plain, single fullered, straight and spear pointed. A removable leather liner applies to this particular sword, dark blue to black, with a red periphery.

Blade length	36.63in (93cm)
Sword weight	1lb 13oz (0.9kg)

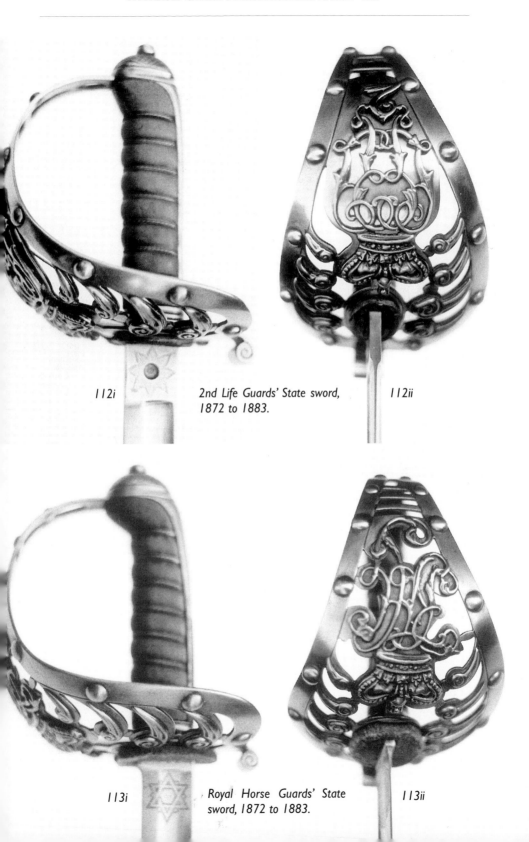

112i   *2nd Life Guards' State sword,*   112ii
1872 to 1883.

113i   *Royal Horse Guards' State*   113ii
sword, 1872 to 1883.

During the period 1832 to 1883 the Household cavalry used the heavy and universal patterns for both officers and rank and file as their service swords; later, from 1887 and 1908-1912 these patterns were also adopted as service swords. There were a few exceptions to this principle, the Household Cavalry Museum acknowledging that some attempts were made to convert state swords into service swords by using steel components. For example the 1832 2nd Life Guards' sword as shown in **Illustrations 114 (i) & (ii)** was manufactured in a different form in which the guard was a diminished form in steel, but the pommel with flaming grenade and bolts of lighting was retained in brass. The blade was changed to a cross section of a shallow wedge and spear pointed, which, unfortunately was not conducive to thrusting. The blade, however, retained all the decoration used on the original and the example shows the sword to have been supplied by Andrews.

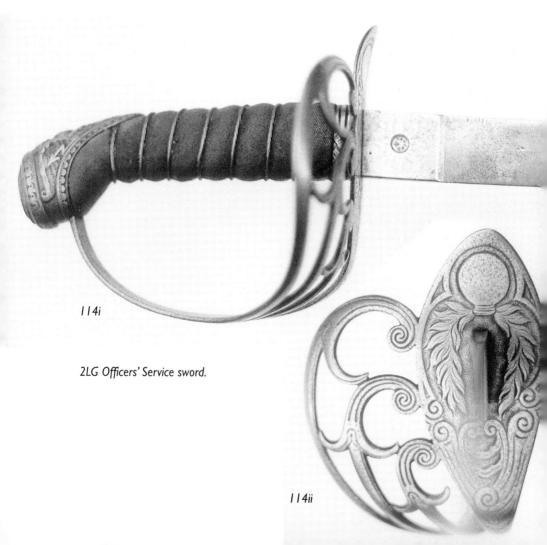

114i

2LG Officers' Service sword.

114ii

The rank and file swords 1832 for the Household Cavalry were generally kept reasonably within the bounds laid down by dress regulations, although it is noticeable, particularly in the War Office reports and minutes, that swords for the Household Cavalry rank and file were always 'special'. They were set apart from the standard patterns in that they had to cater for ceremonial aspects of their functions around the capital and Windsor Castle by virtue of their seniority and precedence within the military hierarchy and their traditional obligations towards guarding the reigning royalty, a precedent created by Charles II. The 1796 pattern Heavy Cavalry disc hilted sword was adopted for service by the Royal Horse Guards in 1802, and by the two Life Guards Regiments in 1812, continuing through to 1832, which seems to have been a general date of change for the Household Cavalry. At that point ceremonial swords were adopted, but could also serve in action.

1st Life Guards' rank and file State sword c. 1832
Illustrations 115i and 115ii

These show the rank and file ceremonial sword of the 1st Life Guards. This sword is based upon the 1821 Heavy Cavalry Troopers' sword with bowl guard but with a broad lined periphery pinned with twelve brass studs in the same manner as for the 1832 Officers' state sword. The forward face of the guard has an upper sword knot aperture and two cutouts coincident and accentuating the etched crown above a scrolled '1 L.G.' The pommel backstrap, with ears, and of smooth steel, is basically the same as the 1821 sword hilt. The grip is fish skin covered without wire binding. The blade is straight, single fullered, spear pointed devoid of decoration and intended for thrusting. There is a single viewing mark on the forté 'Crown/ BN/21'.

Blade length	38.13in (96.3cm)
Sword weight	2lb 6oz (1.1kg)

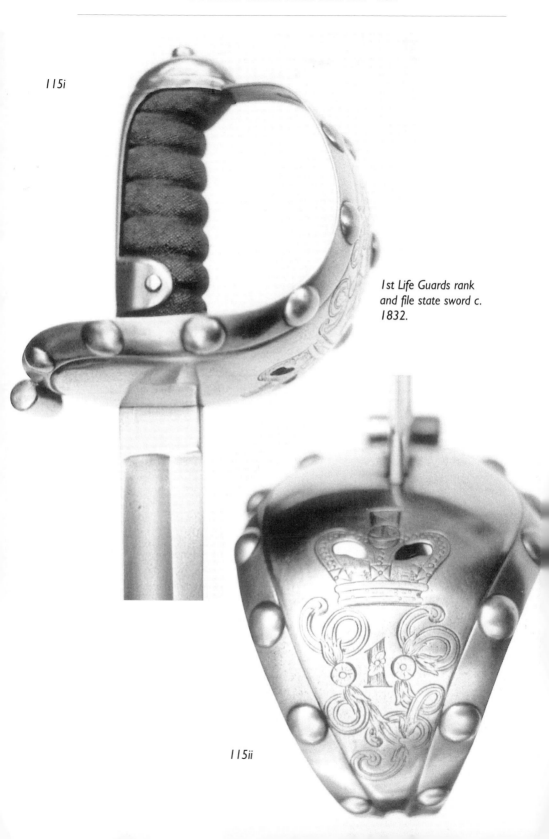

115i

*1st Life Guards rank
and file state sword c.
1832.*

115ii

Until quite recently the equivalent sword for the 2nd Life Guards was not generally known, or recognized as such, and we have to thank Bryan Robson for uncovering this rather spectacular sword. **Illustrations 116 (i) & (ii)** depict the prominent display of the brass representation of a flaming grenade, a distinctive identification of the 2nd Life Guards, a distinction which is further found upon the blade and the hilt of the officers state sword of that period. The 1821 type guard is of thick steel with outer raised rim of twelve brass studs as used in the 1st Life Guards troopers' sword. A rack mark 'C.37' is etched on the guard below the grenade. The pommel/backstrap is of typical 1821 'eared' construction, with a grip covered in black leather, ribbed and devoid of wire binding.

The blade deviates from the usual straight household cavalry blade of the times in that it is curved, single fullered and single edged. The blade is marked 'Enfield', with a few but indistinguishable viewing and inspection marks. This sword is heavily 'weathered', and considerably heavier than other cavalry swords. For state use it would have been admirable, and in service condition it could have been devastating.

Blade length	36.25in (92cm)
Sword weight	2lb 12oz (1.24kg)

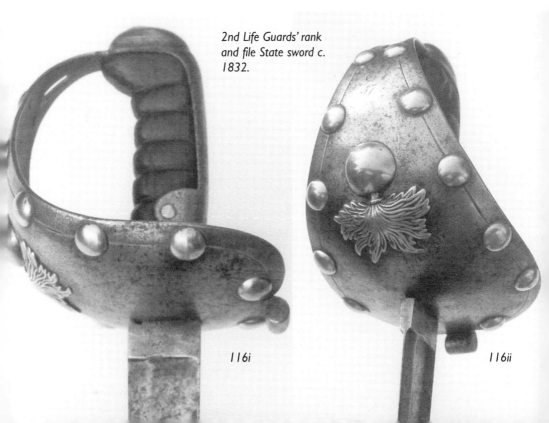

2nd Life Guards' rank and file State sword c. 1832.

116i   116ii

The Royal Horse Guards rank and file sword at that time was that portrayed in Illustration 60, but which may have been in use by some other heavy cavalry regiments. This was due to change, in 1848, to one with a slightly curved blade and a guard with the cut out honeysuckle pattern, but with a brass domed pommel, an adaptation from the 1821 Heavy Cavalry officers' sword. This was subsequently termed the 1848 pattern, and has since been distinguished by its Royal Horse Guard service in Egypt in 1882. The Household Cavalry Museum would define this sword as being used by both Royal Horse Guards and 2nd Life Guards from 1857 to 1885.

The 1880s saw attempts to change all the rank and file swords throughout the British Cavalry, including the Household. An experimental sword was produced in 1881, an example of which was transferred from the Tower to the pattern room at Enfield on the 7 March 1881 for reference, having a Royal Horse Guards seal attached, and also tagged as reference number 579. This sword was not, however, formally sealed as a regulation pattern, being rejected by Colonel F.G. Burnaby of the Royal Horse Guards (probably because the blade was fairly flexible) in favour of the subsequent 1882 Household Cavalry pattern. It is thought that six swords of this type were manufactured for test purposes, each having some slightly different characteristic. The example in the pattern room was listed as: 'Blade 38.75in, Hilt 5³/₄in, with white liner.' The other swords, over time, have passed into other hands, one into the possession of the author as shown in **Illustrations 117 (i) & (ii)**, thought to be number 3 in the series.

For this particular sword the hilt measurement is 6in, the difference from the reference being the brass domed pommel which is ¹/₄" higher. The blade length is 38.68in. The backstrap is eared and retained at the base by a ribbed ferrule, the grip is fish skin covered, bound with a broad raised and lined periphery with the (by now) conventional twelve brass studs. There are separate plain honeysuckle cutouts on the forward and base surfaces of the guard, in line with the 1821 officers' Heavy Cavalry pattern. The blade is straight, single fullered and spear pointed. There are no manufacturing marks, but it does have three pock marks on the back edge. Sword weight is 2lb 10oz (1.19kg).

*Royal Horse Guards'
experimental sword
c. 1881.*

117i

117ii

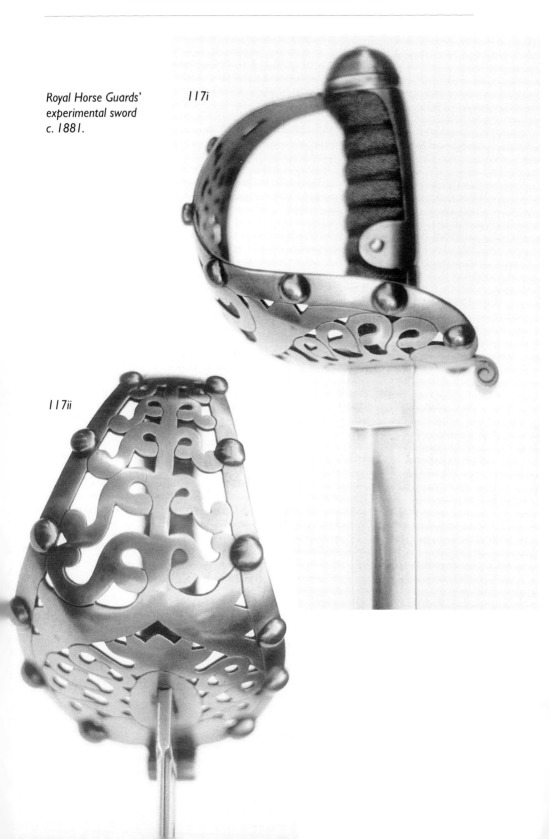

Other research and testing was of course being carried out in line with the 1880 onward investigations and comparisons, the Household Cavalry finally adopting the 1882 pattern Household Cavalry rank and file sword (as opposed to the 1882 universal pattern for other cavalry). This pattern was in two forms, the Mk.I Long with a blade length of 37in and the Mk.I Short with a blade length of 33in. **Illustrations 118 (i) & (ii)** show the common hilt to both these patterns and the basic continuing design for the follow up patterns through to 1892.

For the example shown, the combined pommel backstrap is without ears and is of smoothed steel, the grip being fish skin covered and bound in brass wire. The guard is spread equally either side of the grip, shallow bowled, and has a series of cutouts within the periphery which form a crown above a scrolled 'HC' (for Household Cavalry), within other scrolling, which cannot be termed either honeysuckle, or scroll, or acanthus. The manufacturers mark 'MOLE' is stamped on the guard, either side of the blade entry point, together with one viewing mark 'Crown /B/8'. The blade is a departure from the norm in that it is slightly curved, single fullered and spear pointed, with marks on the forté:

i) WD/Arrow; crown/30/E; obsolete mark; crown/30/E
ii) ' '91' (issue mark); crown/30/E

Blade length	37in (94cm)
Sword weight	2lb 8oz (1.13kg)

Subsequently further changes were made to account for differences in hilt length, blade length and sword weight, producing the:

  a) Household Cavalry sword pattern 1888 Long
  b) Household Cavalry sword pattern 1892 Mk I (1896)
  c) Household Cavalry sword pattern 1892 Mk II (1896), and finally adoption of the service sword to the 1908 universal pattern.

118 (i) & (ii) Household Cavalry universal 1882 pattern.

118i

118ii

New hilt form.

Chapter 15
POMP & WAR

Dress has always been of prime importance to officers of the cavalry, a matter of pride in themselves and in their regiment, and an essential practice passed directly to their men. Witness the Earl of Cardigan who literally spent his annual estate income on his regiment, the 11th Hussars, to ensure that the men were the smartest and most efficient in the British Cavalry. In the earlier days it was inevitable that certainly the officers would adopt special swords to accompany their dress, particularly when posing to have their portraits painted. Many of these swords had hilts in silver and gold inlay, in the form of animals, real or mythical, as in the case of Colonel Alexander Popham's portrait at Littlecote House (1973), which showed his dress sword to have a hilt in the form of a dragon's head; or the more logical seventeenth century small sword sold by Wallis & Wallis in July 2000 which was in the style of Walloon light cavalry swords. The pommel was of inlaid silver depicting flowers and foliage, the base guard of three chased panels depicting warring mounted cavalrymen. Given these leads by the officers it was inevitable that the regiments should adopt a standard form of dress sword for their officers but less ornate; a good example of this being the 3rd Dragoon Guards who are recorded in 1786 as using a standard dress sword with short curved wedge section blade, the hilt all brass cast as a lion's head with a Mameluke type cross quillon, the grip stamped '3 /DG' together with another number that was allocated to a particular officer. In 1796 the dress regulations allowed for Heavy Cavalry officers to wear the type of dress sword shown in **Illustrations 119 (i) & (ii)**, its hilt form based upon a heart shaped shell guard, simple knucklebow and cross quillons. For the sword illustrated, the grip is bound over its length in silver wire, the hilt furniture is gilded copper, the blade is plain, double edged with central fuller having the etched name of the supplier 'J.J. Runkel - Solingen'.

| Blade length | 31.75in (81.2cm) |
| Sword weight | 1lb 12oz (0.8kg) |

It was not unusual to decorate the blade and many good examples with blueing and gilding are to be found.

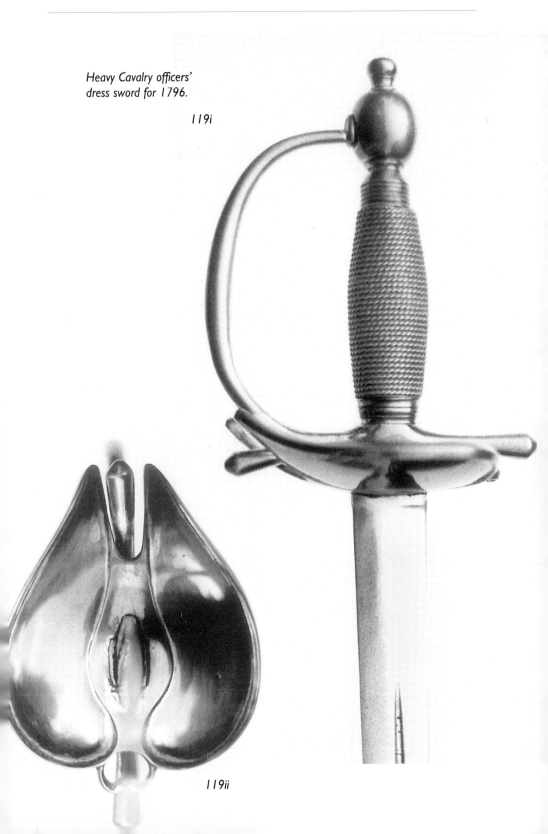

Heavy Cavalry officers' dress sword for 1796.

119i

119ii

A variant of this sword was that used by the Life Guards in which the shell guards are extended up the knucklebow and squared off and the forward quillon raised at an angle, as shown in **Illustrations 120 (i) & (ii)**.

This sword has a grip bound in silver wire, furniture gilded over copper, and the pommel is extended. The blade is single edged, fullered, plain and spear pointed and no manufacturer's mark.

Blade length	35.75in (94.9cm)
Sword weight	1lb 13oz (0.83kg)

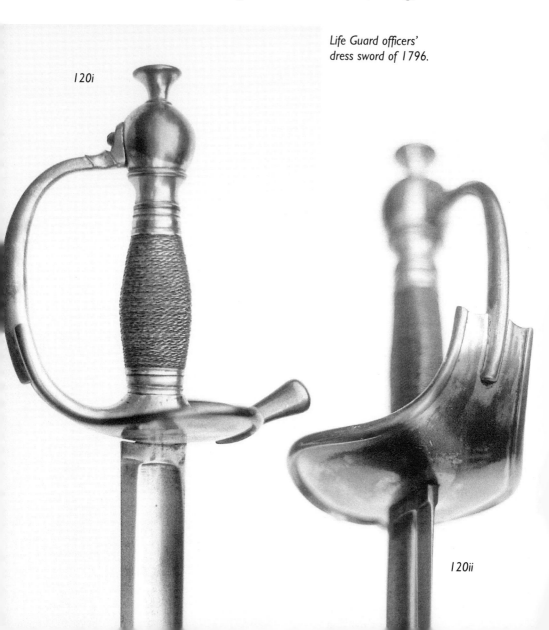

Life Guard officers' dress sword of 1796.

120i

120ii

There does not appear to be a dress sword for the Light Cavalry for the 1796 dress regulations, but it probably took the form of the 1796 Light Cavalry sabre similar to that shown in **Illustrations 121 (i) and (ii).**

This particular dress sword was for a Scottish Regiment, either Cavalry or Infantry, having an ivory grip with silver wire binding, steel furniture of the later 1796 pattern, a wedge shaped curved blade profusely decorated with alternate panels of polished steel and blue gilt, predominantly displaying the Scottish motifs of a lion, thistle, saltire and St Andrew.

Blade length	29in (73.7cm)
Sword weight	1lb 11oz (0.75kg)

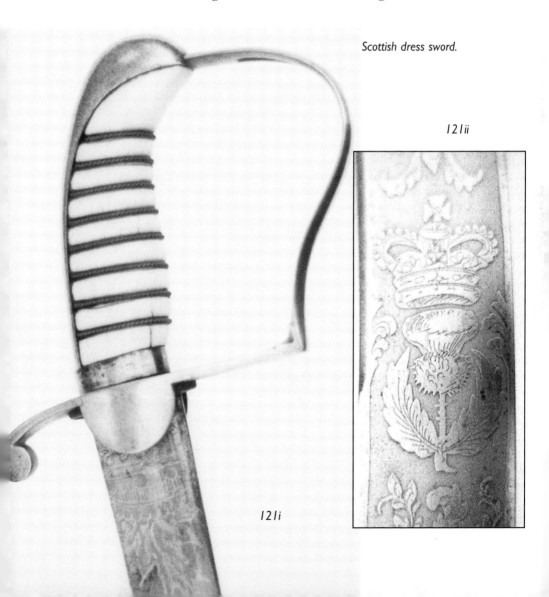

Scottish dress sword.

121 ii

121 i

The Indian Regiments of the time adopted the swords of the dress regulations but some officers deviated with 1796 'type' swords, locally made, in which the grip was of carved ivory similar to that in **Illustration 122**, in which the blade was again wedge shaped, curved and plain.

Blade length	30.5in (77.5cm)
Sword weight	1lb 12oz (0.8kg)

The advantage of these swords was that they were fairly ornate, being covered with silver sheet, and simple decorations, cheaper to produce than British supplied swords, and could double up as a second fighting sword in an emergency.

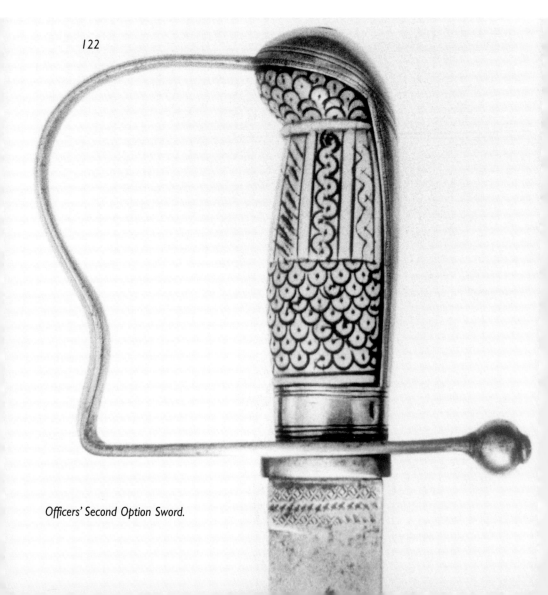

122

Officers' Second Option Sword.

About 1825 the form of the dress sword changed to that of the Mameluke hilted sabre for both Heavy and Light Cavalry regiments, the first forms following the slightly curved pipe backed blades of the 1821 Cavalry Officers' patterns, but changing later to wedge section blades that afford more surface for extensive decoration. **Illustration 123** shows a typical early Mameluke hilted dress sword with pipe backed blade, simple in its presentation of carved ivory grip and floral decoration to the cross quillons and over the width of the blade tang.

Blade length	32.25in (81.9cm)
Sword weight	1lb 12oz (0.8kg)

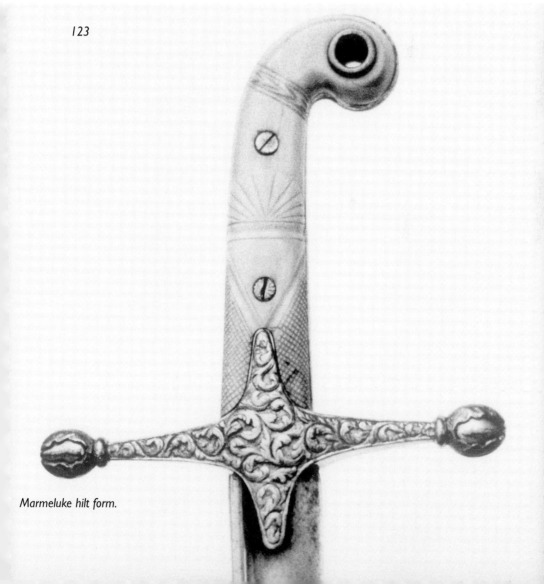

123

Marmeluke hilt form.

The only instances where rank and file were allowed a form of dress sword were in the regimental bands, and then purely for ceremonial activities: reviews, receiving honours, trooping the colour, beating retreat, changing the guard, funerals and coronations. Although the prerogative for ceremony was that of the Household Cavalry, the other cavalry regiments were not without their own brand of splendour when put to the occasion.

Illustration 124 is of a Scottish regiment, the 2nd Dragoons, or the Royal North British Dragoons as it was known in its earlier days. The all brass hilt portrays a lion's head with flowing mane and scaled body grip, over Mameluke cross quillons with central circular device of a thistle within the motto 'NEMO ME IMMUNE LACESSIT'. The blade is curved, fullered, plain without any marking, and capable of being used as a cutting weapon in an emergency. A copper chain, in place of a knucklebow, runs from the mouth of the lion to a forward quillon.

> Blade length 27.75in (70.5cm)
> Sword weight 1lb 9oz (0.7kg)

Illustration 125 shows a band sword attributed to the Household Cavalry, again with a lion's head in brass and gilding, extending down the backstrap, the favoured cross quillon guard being surmounted by a crown. The blade is slightly curved and 25in long.

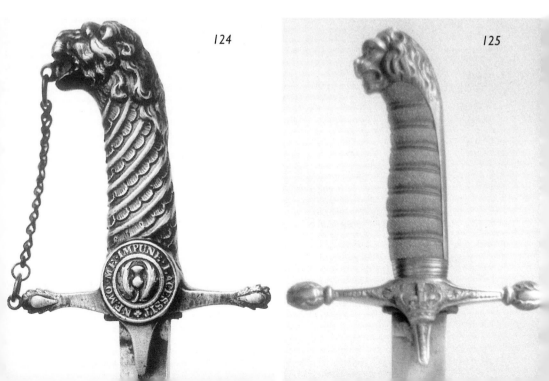

124

125

The ceremonial aspects of the capital and Windsor Castle were the prerogative of the Household Cavalry due to their precedence and seniority, and their allegiance to the Royal Family since the times of Charles II, and perhaps before. Ceremony and pomp is a dedication in itself and needs the commitment of men and officers who can excel in it, both in times of peace and times of war. Such a man of commitment and dedication, particularly to his regiment, was Francis Mountjoy Martyn, born in 1809 in India of a dedicated military family and joining the 2nd Life Guards as Second Lieutenant in 1827. By chance this regiment saw little overseas activity, or conditions of war, during the next thirty years, spending its time between ceremonial duties at Buckingham Palace, Knightsbridge and Windsor Castle, and partaking in riot suppression in support of the local yeomanry in various parts of the country. This was convenient to F.M. Martyn who was advancing himself socially and in his career through the high society that moved around the capital and royal circles, acquiring properties in Belgravia and near Windsor Castle to ensure that his alternating duties in these areas could be undertaken in a dedicated manner and reasonably trouble free. Regularly taking his promotions by purchase or brevet within the regiment, he became Lieutenant Colonel in 1857 and Brevet Colonel in 1858, finally retiring in 1863. Life, however was not entirely 'spit and polish' (never a Martyn forté by itself). He participated in those areas of riot suppression throughout the country, and in particular at Kennington Common in 1848, but finding time for social alliance with Lizzie Howard, for whom he set up house and servants in St Johns Wood, until she wandered off into the arms of the future Napoleon III, earning herself a title and a small château in France in doing so. His ceremonial activities however were many and varied and outweighed his social life. He could account for living in the reign of three sovereigns, attending the funeral of George IV, the coronation and funeral of William IV and the coronation of Victoria, the funerals of Prince Albert and the Duke of Wellington, each with their appropriate degree of pomp and ceremony and preparation. He eventually retired to watch his string of racehorses win, or lose, and left his state swords of 1810 and 1832 hanging on the wall.

And so to war, a state in which the British Cavalry excelled as no other. To show their pride in their regiments' achievements and honours, the officers began to record the regiments' titles and battle honours upon their swords, a process which really began with the age of the 1821 pattern. Many examples can be found, the following are but a few.

Illustrations 126 (i), (ii) and (iii) – The honours recorded on this sword of Captain Archmond of the 3rd Dragoon Guards, 1821 pattern, are: Talavera, Vittoria, Albuhera, and Peninsula, together with the regimental motif of Prince of Wales feathers, and 'The Prince of Wales 3rd Dragoon Guards', in a garter. The officers' crest of an eagle and motto, *Spes Lucis Eterne* with the initials RHA are embossed on the blade towards the guard.

Sword of a 3rd Dragoon Guards officer c. 1863.

127i   127ii

Sword of a 9th Lancer officer.

Illustrations 127 (i) and (ii) show an 1821 pattern sword of the 9th Queen's Royal Lancers, the battle honours of 'Peninsula' and 'Punniar' below the regimental cipher of 'IX' between crossed lances. The officer's crest of a unicorn head below the motto *Dum Spiro Spero* is the only indication of his origins.

Illustrations 128 (i), (ii) and (iii) show an 1821 pattern sword of Lieutenant Colonel John Miller of the 13th Hussars (Light Dragoons), previously of the 3rd Dragoon Guards, and bears the battle honours: Peninsular, Waterloo, Alma, Balaclava, Inkerman, and Sevastapol, below a garter with the motto *Viret in Aeternum* about '13th'. John Miller was eventually to achieve the rank of Major General in the British Cavalry.

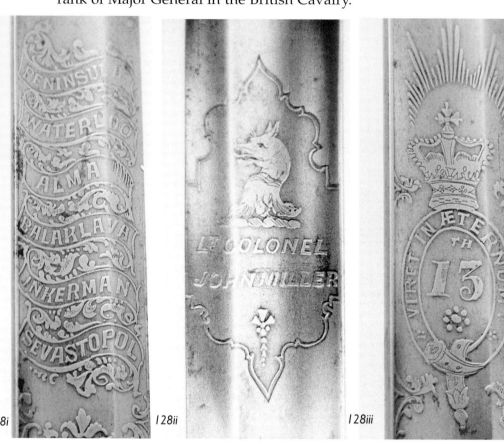

128i   128ii   128iii

Sword of Lieutenant Colonel John Miller.

Illustrations 129 (i) and (ii) of an unknown officer's sword of 1821 pattern, but bearing the motto *Aut Cursu Aut Cominis Armis* below the crown, and a wreath of battle honours embossed about the regimental cipher of 'Queens XVI Lancers' with crossed lances:

Talavera, Fuente d'Onor, Vittoria, Salamanca, Nive, Peninsula, Waterloo, Burtpore, Chunzee, Alival, Afghanistan, Maharajpore, and Sobraon.

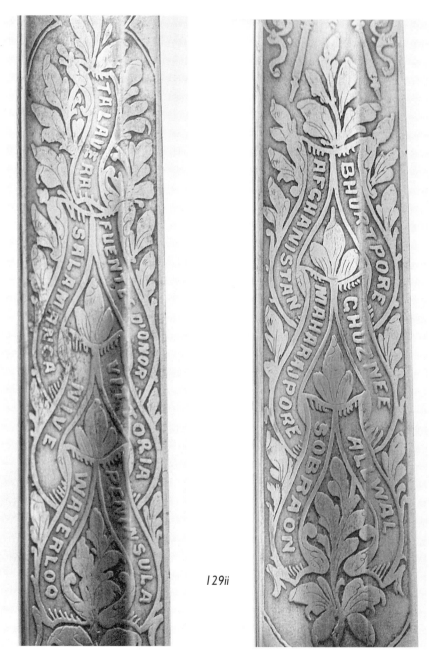

129i   129ii

16th Lancers battle honours.

130i

130ii

18th Hussars' sword.

Crest of F.A. Baines.

Illustrations 130 (i) and (ii) The sword of F.A. Baines of 1821 pattern, bearing an embossed cipher of the XVIII Hussars within a garter, with the battle honours of Peninsula and Waterloo, and the family crest of a leopard rising from a coronet.

The men and officers were not lacking 'dash' or courage, or flinched from the prospect of death, and that is well borne out by the many battle honours seen above, often shared with other regiments. We can also show the case of a few individual officers. Edward Kelly had exchanged from the 1st Royal Dragoons to the 1st Life Guards in 1810, and as a captain served with them in the Peninsular in 1813, following through to Waterloo in 1815. Despite the rigours of that enforced campaign he distinguished himself at Grenappe, the day before Waterloo, leading the 1st Life Guard charge against the French Lancers du Garde on three occasions, killing the Lancer Colonel and earning the recommendation of Lord Uxbridge to the Duke of Wellington.

On the following day at Waterloo he further distinguished himself in the Household Cavalry charge having three horses disabled under him, sustaining a severe gun shot wound to his leg. For his actions he was awarded Brevet Major, mentioned in dispatches, and received several decorations both British and foreign. His undoubted courage was enhanced in that his actions were effected, not with a heavy cavalry sword, but with a pipe backed light cavalry sabre of the 16th Queen's Light Dragoons by Prosser, duly blued and gilt decorated with the cipher of the 16th Queen's Light Dragoons and a stand of arms. Charles Hyde Villiers showed a valour of a different kind against a waiting Boer ambush of perhaps several thousand men. In the first charge against the Boers at Kragersdorp sixty were either killed, wounded or taken prisoner, causing the men following Jameson on his raid into an enforced *laager*, with no prospects of re-enforcements arriving from Johannesburg as promised, but with Boer re-enforcements seen to be readily pouring into the area. Withering fire during the night must have indicated that the end was near, forcing them into a running fight the next morning to Doornkop, where they finally surrendered against insuperable odds. The final count was seventeen killed (three officers), fifty-five wounded, thirty-five missing. Rhodes, the engineer of this debacle, had a laconic reaction to the losses: 'Well, it is a little history being made, that is all'. Finally, we have that anonymous Victorian officer whose intent was well and truly embossed upon his sword for all to see and know, and shared by many others:

A strong hand to bear me for England to fight.

LIST OF REGIMENTS

This list only covers those Regiments noted in this book, and by their names used for the period discussed. They are not in order of military precedence and do not comprise the total content of the British Army at any one time:-

REGIMENT

Artillery, Royal.
Dragoons,   1st Royal
        ,   2nd Royal North British
        ,   3rd Kings Own Light
        ,   4th Royal Irish
        ,   5th Royal Irish Light
        ,   6th Iniskillings
        ,   7th Queens Own Light
        ,   10th Prince of Wales Own
                Royal Regiment of Light
        ,   15th The Kings Light
        ,   16th Light
        ,   17th Light
        ,   30th Light
        ,   Canadian
Dragoon Guards,   2nd The Queens
        ,   3rd Prince of Wales
        ,   4th Royal Irish
        ,   5th Princess Charlotte of Wales's
        ,   6th Carabiniers
        ,   7th The Princess Royals
Cameron Highlanders,   Queens Own.
Engineers, Royal
French 105th Regiment of the Line
Horse Grenadier Guards
Household Cavalry, 1st Lifeguards
        , 2nd Lifeguards
        , Royal Horse Guards.
Hussars, 4th Queens Own
        , 10th Prince of Wales Own
        , 11th Prince Alberts Own
        , 13th
        , 18th
        , 20th
        , 25th
Lancers , 9th Queens Royal
        , 16th Queens

, 17th Duke of Cambridge's Own
Light Cavalry, 33rd (Indian)
Mounted Infantry, East Kent
Yeomanry, City of London (Rough Riders)
        , Earl of Chesters (Cavalry)
        , Hampshire (Carabiniers)
        , Imperial
        , Lanark and Dumfries Regiment of
                South African Light Horse
        , Shropshire (Cavalry)
        , Warwick Light Dragoons
        , Warwickshire (Cavalry)

LIST OF PERSONALITIES AND ORGANIZATIONS

NAME	FUNCTION
à Court, Charles	ADC to General Buller.
Albert, Prince	Consort to Queen Victoria
Archmond	Captain, 3rd Dragoon Guards
Austin & Oaker	Supplier of Uniforms & Swords
Baines, F.A.	An Officer of the 18th Hussar's
Barlow	Colonel of a Cavalry Regiment
Barrett, C.R.B.	Military Author
Bland	Supplier of Uniforms & Swords
Bleckmann	German Supplier of Swords
Buller	General of British Boer War Troops
Burdett Coutts, Baroness	Patron of the Arts
Byron	Lord
Cater, F.J.	Supplier of Swords
Chambers	Supplier of Uniforms & Swords
Charles I	A King of Great Britain
Charles II	A King of Great Britain
Cooper & Banks	Supplier of Swords
Cromwell, William	Civil War General (Parliamentarion) Later Lord Protector
Cumberland	Duke, son of George II
Curzon, George A.	Lt. Colonel of the Lifeguards.
Dawes, N & S	Suppliers of Swords
De Vere, Aubrey	1st Earl of Oxford
Fairfax	Civil War General (Parliamentarian)
Farara, Andrea	Swordsmith much imitated
Ffoulkes, Charles	Military Author
Firths	Steel Supplier

Franklin   Agent for arms

Gill, Thomas   Supplier of Swords
Gilpin   Civilian Sword Supplier

Hamburger & Rogers   Military Outfitter
Hanmer, Sir Edward   Major, R.H.G.
Hanmer, Henry   Major, R.H.G.
Harvey, Samuel   A family of Sword Suppliers
Hopkinson   Co-author with Ffoulkes
Howard, Lizzie   Consort to Maj (Lt. Col) F.M. Martyn
Hesketh   One time owners of Rufford Old Hall
Hor, Willem   Dutch Sword Blade maker

Innes-Kerr, Alexandrina   Wife of C.H. Villiers

Jameson, Dr. Leander Starr   Perpetrator of the Jameson Raid
Jessel, Herbert Merton   Captain, 17th Lancers, et al

Kelly, Edward   Major, 1st Lifeguards
Kempson, C.H.   Lieutenant, 1st Royal dragoons
King, Bolton   Major, Warwickshire Yeo. Cavalry

Longford, Elizabeth   Military Biographical Authoress

Martyn, Francis Mountjoy   Lt. Col. 2nd Lifeguards
Miller, John   Lt. Col. 13th Hussars
Mole, Robert   Supplier of Swords
Mungeam, G.I.   Military author

Neumann, George C.   American Military author
Nicholls, William Devereux   Lt. Earl of Chesters Yeomanry Cavalry
Norman, A.V.B.   Military author

Osborn & Gunby   Supplier of Swords

Pakenham, Thomas   Military author
Partridge, Noel   Captain, Hampshire Carabinieres
Popham, Alexander   Colonel portrayed at Littlecote House
Prosser   Sword Supplier

Reeves   Sword Supplier
Rhodes, Cecil   Originator of the Jameson Raid and
                                            Founder of Rhodesia

Robson, Brian   Author of Military Arms
Runkel, J.J.   Supplier of Swords

Sandersons   Steel Suppliers
Sinclair   16th Century supplier of swords

Tarleton, Banastre   Loyalist commander in American
                                            War of Independence
Thurkle   Supplier of Swords

Travers, Augustus W.   Lt. 5th Dragoon Guards

Uxbridge, Lord   Commanding Cavalry in Napoleonic War

Villiers, Charles Hyde   Major R.H.G. in Jameson raid

Walker, Samuel   Recipient of a prize sword
Wallis & Wallis   Specialist Auctioneers, Military Arms
Wellington, Duke of   Overall Commander of British Armies
                                    In the Napoleonic War
Wilkinson, Fredrick   Military author
Wilkinson, Henry   Sword Supplier
Wilkinson-Latham   Military author
Wolsternholme   One time family of Nostell Priory

BIBLIOGRAPHY

Blackmore, David, *Arms and Armour of the English Civil Wars*, Royal
    Armouries, 1990

Ffoulkes, Charles, *Arms & Armament*, George G. Harrap & Co. Ltd, 1945/47

Ffoulkes, Charles & E. C. Hopkinson, *Sword Lance and Bayonet*, Arco Publishing
    Co. Inc, 1938/1967

May, Lieutenant Commander W. E., and P. G. W Annis, *Swords for Sea
    Service*, (in 2 volumes. Refer to part IV of Volume 2 for Sword
    Cutlers and Proof Marks with dates of operation in Great
    Britain), HMSO, London, 1970

Neumann, George C., *Swords and Blades of the American Revolution*,
    David & Charles (Holdings) Ltd, 1973
    – *The History of Weapons of the American Revolution*,
    Harper & Row (Publishers of New York, Evanston and London), 1967

Robson, Brian, *Swords of the British Army – The Regulation Patterns of 1788
    – 1914, The Revised Edition*, National Army Museum, 1996
    (The recognized current authority on British Army Swords)

Wagner, Edward, *Cut and Thrust Weapons*, Spring Books, 1967

Wallace John, *Scottish Swords and Dirks*, Arms & Armour Press Ltd/Lionel
    Leventhal Ltd, *1970*

Walter, John, *The Sword & Bayonet Makers of Imperial Germany 1871-1918*,
    (Useful references to the marks used by some German suppliers
    to Great Britain), Lyon Press/Arms & Armour Press Ltd/ Lionel
    Leventhal Ltd, 1973

Wilkinson/Latham, R. J., *Pictorial History of Swords and Bayonets*, Ian Allan Ltd., 1973

Wilkinson/Latham, John, *British Cut and Thrust Weapons*, David & Charles
    Publications Ltd, 1971

Wilkinson, Frederic, *Edged Weapons*, Guinness Signatures, 1970
    Swords and Daggers, Ward, Locke & Co. Ltd, 1967

Wilkinson/Latham, John, *British Military Swords – from 1800 to the Present Day*,
    Hutchinson & Co. Ltd, 1966

Wise, T., *European Edged Weapons*, Almark Publishing Co. Ltd, 1974